TABLE OF CO[N]

M000170271

For my kids and grandkids.

Author's Note

When I was growing up, I was able to experience a lot of different things in life – poverty, a single parent household, sexual abuse from someone outside the family and a half absent father. I could've let my circumstances define me and direct my life. But I didn't. I'm living proof of what happens when you consciously choose to be a product of your decisions, as opposed to falling victim to your circumstances.

My positive choices led me to become a football player, a vacuum salesman, a corrections officer, a football coach, a *good* police officer and the founder of the Be A Better Me Foundation.

As a police officer, I've dealt with all types of crimes and criminals, from petty theft to sexual assaults and murder. I've experienced people in my community at their highest of highs and lowest of lows. Through community policing and my foundation, I'm starting to see many more highs than lows. It starts with our youth.

I'm here to make a difference in the lives of every kid I meet. Kids with bad family situations, who feel like they can't talk to anybody. That's why I'm here today. I use all of my experiences to connect with kids and help them shape better lives. Some of them do not have a blueprint, so I make sure they get one.

Through all the trials and tribulations, I know that I'm right where I'm supposed to be. This is my calling, not pro-football as I had once hoped. My calling is this thing that I'm building. I can help more people doing this than I could playing football in front of hundreds of thousands of people.

I'm just an average dude who grew up on the 'wrong side of the tracks.' I changed my path and now I get to spread positivity to our youth and community. The lives that I've impacted are proof that maybe, just maybe, all we need is a little more hope and love in this world.

I became the change I wanted to see and I truly hope this book helps you do the same. Thank you for all of your support throughout the years.

In Memory of
Clinton Sr, Elnora, Mary,
Lloyd, and Charlene

"It is your reaction to adversity, not the adversity itself, that determines how your life's story will develop."

– Dieter F. Uchtdorf

PART

I

ADVERSITY

CHAPTER 1

THE STRUGGLE WAS REAL

Childhood

I grew up in a rough neighborhood in Akron, Ohio.

When I was born, my mom and dad both worked at BFGoodrich. They each made around $17 an hour, which was really good pay back in the day, especially when gas only cost about 80 cents a gallon. When I was very young, my parents did a great job providing for me and my siblings. But, even at an early age, it seemed the odds were stacked against me.

When I was two or three years old, a doctor had to break my legs and put me in braces, fearing that I wouldn't be able to walk or run right. For eight months, I had to wear corrective shoes with bars attached to the side of them. My mom remembers lying me in bed, staring down at me and crying as I laid there looking helpless and unable to move. As a parent, she wished it happened to her instead of me.

My mom kept those braces and shoes for a while. I actually remember the image of them in the corner of my room more than I remember wearing them. Years later, I would watch *Forrest Gump* and see him in leg braces, thinking to myself, *Man, that was me!*

Because of my legs, I felt slower than other kids. On top of that, I was a very husky. When I played football or basketball with kids in the neighborhood, I would either be the last one picked or I wouldn't get picked at all.

When I was four or five, my pediatrician discovered that I had a small hole in my heart and I was diagnosed with a heart murmur. The doctor said that it could go one of two ways: it could either open and grow, or it could close on its own. My mom was devastated, again. When we got to the car, she started crying and praying that her son would be healed. About a year later, the hole in my heart closed and I had a normal heartbeat. From that day on, my mother went to church faithfully. My mother had always attended church, but from that day on, she attended attended church every single Sunday. With her, there are two guarantees, she's going to brush her teeth and she's going to go to church.

In addition to braces on my legs and a heart murmur, I had asthma and had to carry an inhaler up until my freshman year of high school.

Amazingly, after all those childhood complications, I became one of the biggest and fastest kids in my neighborhood. I played football from the time I was eight years old until I was 30.

Riches to Rags

When I was seven or so, my parents got divorced. Just like that, we were poor. My dad left my mother for another woman, who went on to become his wife and my stepmother. Ultimately, my siblings and I were the ones left suffering once the dust settled. We went from having Christmas and birthday presents every year to having nothing at all. After the divorce, we never had another birthday party during our childhood. For the next few years, there was endless arguing, fighting and court battles between my mom and dad.

To make matters worse, my mom got laid off from BFGoodrich. We had our lights and water cut off a few times, sometimes boiling pots of water just to take a bath. We were in trouble. I don't know how we kept our house as long as we did. My mom started going to school while working two jobs. My grandparents would stay over and watch us while my mom worked at Dunkin Donuts in the middle of the night and attended college during the day. Even with my mom putting in all this effort, we were unable to keep up with the bills.

We never knew where our next meal would come from. Many years later, when I graduated from high school, I received an award for having perfect attendance for nine consecutive years. From someone else's perspective, it may be considered a major accomplishment to go to school and learn without missing a day for so many years in a row. From my perspective, perfect attendance meant that I had a guaranteed meal every day for nine years.

I just remember my mom struggling all the time. There were times when I would hear her in another room crying because times had gotten so tough. Looking back, my mother was a truly amazing woman and mother. Her resiliency was like no other. As much as I appreciate her and everything she did for me, there were times when I wanted to rebel against how she raised us. She was always the disciplinarian.

Children can sense tension between divorced parents and will try to manipulate the situation. It is common for kids take their anger out on the parent who is constantly there for them and put the other on a pedestal.

One day, I got in trouble for something. Shamefully, I remember saying, "I wish I lived with my dad."

I didn't think my mom heard me, but she came into the living room and started packing up a few of my things. "Ok," she said, "let's go, so you can go live with your dad!" During that time in my life, I really didn't want to live with my dad, and she knew it. I broke down crying and got my act together really quick.

Measuring Up
Our refrigerator usually contained a jug of water, a container of spoiled milk, some butter, government cheese, maybe a loaf of stale bread-ends and we always had a bottle of cod liver oil. It was a struggle. For a short time, my mom was using food stamps and I remember our family eating blackeye peas or pinto beans four or five nights a week. I was getting older

and started comparing our lifestyle to other people around the neighborhood. We were in this gang infested area and I'm seeing everybody out there hustling, selling drugs and gangbanging. I'm not going to lie, it was intriguing. I wanted nice clothes. I wanted to help my mother, so she didn't have to struggle anymore. I wanted nice stuff, too.

When I was in public places with other kids, I had a lot of anxiety because I knew people were going to pick on me for not having nice things. At that time, everybody else was rocking Adidas and Kangol. And there I was walking around in Wrangler jeans and cheap plastic shoes. Back in the day, Rolling Acres Mall or O J Men's & Boy's Wear were the places to shop. Unfortunately, our budget was more like Woolworth's. But if it wasn't on the clearance rack, we couldn't get it. My mother made sure to stretch every penny we had on school clothes and supplies. In gym class, all the other kids' shoes would squeak because they had name brand shoes. I did not have that luxury. My mom bought me Pro Wings and Sprint shoes. When I played, my shoes sounded like I was wearing high heeled stilettos.

That was a big deal for me as a teenager. I didn't want to be around people, because I didn't have the things they did. But I did find comfort by hanging out with some of my friends who were also poor. That was my comfort zone, where I could be me and have fun. Even to this day, I feel like it affects me to a small extent. People and kids always ask me why I wear sunglasses all the time.

Me and my sister, Lanell.

Honestly, I still wear glasses to cover the pain I see in my eyes when I look in the mirror at times. The feeling that everyone I encounter can also see my shame and embarrassment.

A lot of those feelings came from watching my mom struggle. That was the biggest thing I had to overcome. She did the best she could, but sometimes, your best doesn't appear to be good enough. I know what it's like. I see this exact situation every day, where people are working hard, but some situations are overwhelming. It's not easy to hold a job and maintain your kids.

I could have easily been that guy
who was locked up or dead.
Absolutely. I could be that guy today.

The Anger Overtook Me

There was one kid who I remember picking on me a lot. He was a grade above me and had been held back a couple of times. I, on the other hand, had started school early and was the youngest kid in my class. So, this kid had a few years on me. This dude loved to pick on me about my clothes and shoes, and bullying me because I played the violin. But one day, it went too far.

As usual, he started picking on me. I ignored him and he shoved me. I was so furious that I shoved him back as hard as I could. He looked at me in disbelief. Then he said something I will never forget.

"I'm going to beat your ass right after school!"

I was so amped up and angry that I didn't realize the severity of what was yet to come. But when all the kids in school, who were also scared of him, started saying how I was going to die after school, I started to get the picture. My anger wouldn't allow me to be afraid. Plus, in my hood, showing fear would cost you a lifetime of humiliation. I had no choice but to fight. When school let out, all the kids followed me to see me die by the hands of this grown-ass man-child, but when I walked out of school, he was nowhere to be found. It was like a ton of bricks was lifted off my shoulders!

As I continued to walk home, I reached my last turn, Hart Street. There he was, standing with six of his friends. His shirt was off and he was bouncing around like a pro boxer, warming up before a big match. Everyone there was super hyped and ready to witness my death. I tried to walk by him nonchalantly, as if he wasn't even there. But, of course, that didn't work. He ran up on me with his fists up, ready to go.

It was fight or flight time. So, I dropped my violin and went to work. To my surprise, I was holding my own in the fight. The one thing that willed me through that fight was the anger that had been building inside of me from everything else going on in my life. My anger was keeping me alive for the time being, but then the fight took a turn for the worse.

His homeboys started flashing pocket knives and yelling, "Slice his ass!"

My focus turned from the fight to the thought of getting stabbed and actually dying on Hart Street. All I could think about were those kids flashing those knives. A couple of my friends were yelling, "Put the knives away and let them fight!" But all I could think about was being murdered, right then and there.

Bam! Right in the mouth.

The kid hit me as hard as he could and slammed me on the ground. I threw my hands up, laying on the ground and bleeding. The fight was over. The kid and his buddies walked away, and I walked home, quickly and angrily. When I got home, I unlocked the front door, grabbed a knife from the kitchen and ran outside. I was ready to find all of them and cut their entire crew with my mom's kitchen knife. If I knew where they were at that moment, I would probably be writing this story from prison.

I cooled down, but the anger and feelings of inadequacy were still there. Also, looking back, I really loved playing the violin. And I was good. But being picked on by that bully, in part for playing violin, caused me to quit playing. That's something I regret to this day.

Street Cred

Even though we couldn't pay our bills at that time, we were still living in a big house in the hood, so everyone always thought we were rich. And for years, I put on this charade like we were. One day, my mother wanted me to run to a local corner store, Rocky's, to get some bread and eggs. She handed me some food stamps and sent me on my way. My mission was to get in and out of the store as quickly as possible. As I was crossing the street to Rocky's, six members of the Eastside 9 Kings gang came out of the store. Instantly, I was scared. When you encounter a gang on the street, the fight or flight response gets real, quick.

Because of the anger I had inside of me, fighting one or two wasn't a huge issue, but fighting six would have been a death sentence. But some of these dudes were older and had beards. I wasn't even sure if I had reached puberty yet. Next thing you know, one of the gang members yelled out to me, "Sharpe, come here!" The leader of this gang was that dude on the streets! Him and his brothers were notorious for beating the brakes off dudes young and old in the hood.

I was too close to them and too far away from home to make a run for it. A few of these guys were the same group of dudes that surrounded me and my friends a couple of years earlier. One of the guys karate roundhouse-kicked my friend in the face, sending his glasses soaring in the air. I was already in flight mode before his glasses hit the ground. I ran through the projects to Joy Park Rec and survived another day from gang violence. I never felt so lucky before in my life. So back on this day, I felt like my luck had run out! With my heart in my throat, I walked towards them sizing up which one of them I would need to punch before I ran. I slowly put my hand in my pocket and placed my house key between my knuckles.

The gang leader said "Sharpe, I see you doing your thing on the football field and basketball court. Keep doing your thing 'cause there isn't nothing in these streets for you. And if you need anything or anyone bothers you, you let me know."

Then he dapped me up and I rushed in the store, panicked and relieved at the same time. In my neighborhood, this is not how encounters with gang members went. I was so shocked that they didn't beat me down that I almost forgot what my mom sent me to the store for. That encounter let me know that I was special and that I had a positive pass in my hood.

The Lure of the Streets

One day when I was about 11, I was outside tossing my football in the yard when a local drug dealer called me over, "Young blood, come on over here."

I walked over, but I kept my distance because I knew this dude was a dealer. "What's up," I said.

"You want to make some money?" He asked. And I'm like, "Yeah."

"I'm gonna give you 80 bucks," he said.

That was some serious money for a little kid. "Okay, so what do I gotta do?" I asked. "I want you to deliver this package for me," he replied.

Somewhere inside, I knew what he was going to ask me to do. Even though I said yes at first, I quickly processed it over in my head.

"Man, I can't," I said, "My mom is gonna be home and I have to go to church with her."

He shook his head, "Get out of here, you little sucker."

He just kind of dogged me. That was one of the most defining moments of my life. I realized then that if I would've delivered that package, at some point, I could have ended up getting shot or getting arrested. And my whole life would've changed for the worse.

I'm the oldest kid in my family, but I don't think I was much of a protector or anything back then, because it was more about survival. I was just trying to survive in that neighborhood. I mean, I looked out for my brother and sister, but at the same time my friends and I used to pick on my sister a lot. I feel bad now, but it could've been much worse. My brother and sister kept their noses clean, and I think it was because they were so young by the time we moved out of that neighborhood. I think I helped them stay on the right path more than I actually kept them out of trouble. I suppose if anything, I was a positive role model because I wasn't out being a punk.

But that neighborhood was so bad. There was angst, stress, pressure and madness everywhere. Being exposed to all that madness taught me more than I'd ever imagined. Constantly hearing gunshots – every day and night – and trying my best to avoid fights. In a way, the hood motivated me to want something different in my life.

Boy n the Hood
Although street life didn't appeal to me, neither did the police. In my neighborhood, even some of the police were bad dudes. There were a lot of cops in the area who were known for jacking people up, with or without cause. And it wasn't really a race thing. Sure, white cops would give me the eye, but even the black cops would drive by and mean-mug me while I was throwing a ball in my front yard. I've seen officers tightening their gloves and staring me down while they drove by my house. They were just waiting for me to do something wrong. They looked at every young black man in our neighborhood as trouble. When I was young, I even heard rumors that some officers would take you out to the

area of the Goodyear blimp hangar and tune you up if they felt you needed it.

In all actuality, there was trouble everywhere. My mama used to tell me, "You better not leave our yard." So, I'd spend a lot of time in my yard throwing my football up in the air and catching it. I got picked on a lot for not being able to leave my yard. My mom didn't really want me to be in the deep heart of the projects, but I would go there anyways because that's where all my friends lived. When my mom would allow me to venture off, I knew to be home before the street lights came on. Or else!

One day after school, my friends and I were at the wrong place at the wrong time. A fight broke out with some guys nearby and we knew those guys fought with knives and guns. We left the area as quickly as possible. We took the longest way home possible, trying to avoid any danger or involvement with anything that was going on that night.

As we were navigating our way back home, a cruiser rolled up on the curb in front of us and scared the hell out of us. The cops got out of the car; one had his gun out and the other had his hand on his gun.

"Get on the car. Put your hands on the car!"

They threw me and my friends on the car – almost exactly like that scene in *Boyz n the Hood* when the cops threw Ricky on the car.

So, I'm laying on the car and shaking. In my head, I was like, *Yo, what is going on? I didn't even do anything. This is wild.* The officers ran us for warrants and checked us for weapons. It was a traumatic experience, but we weren't doing anything wrong, so they had to let us go. This was another defining moment of my youth that just fueled more anger and rage on top of what I had been dealing with in my life. I couldn't connect to peers, thugs or the local police.

Bad Boys

A lot of my history with the police had been bad. It wasn't until high school that I started seeing the police as people, when an officer approached me to talk about my basketball skills. He treated me with respect and kindness, which changed my perspective. Up until then, my perspective of all police officers was negative.

Finally, I started to see police in a different light. Here was this completely normal dude, unlike all the other officers I encountered or heard about. This one experience helped me learn that you can't group people so generally, whether they be the police or anyone else. It doesn't make sense to say that *all* police officers are bad. The number of good officers out there certainly outweighs the number of bad ones.

Looking back on things, the officers who worked in my neighborhood were missing huge opportunities to get out of their cruisers and build relationships with me and other kids around the neighborhood. The distrust that I had for officers could have been squashed with just one simple act of kindness. Later in my life, I would start using this lesson in everything that I did.

Kindness would prevail.

Middle School LaMar.

CHAPTER 2

GUIDING LIGHTS

A Family Treasure
Sadly, not every child has the luxury of getting to know their grandparents, but I was lucky to have relationships with mine over the course of my childhood. I am very grateful for the time that I was able to spend with my grandparents. They helped mold me into the person I am today. My mother's parents were the best source of love that any person could ask for. My grandmother Elnora took us to school from time to time and gave me some of the best advice I've ever receive in life during those trips. And, boy, could she cook! My grandfather Clinton taught me the value of hard work, which is something I have carried with me all my life. He would pick me up at 6 a.m. and take me to our favorite breakfast spot, Ann's Restaurant in Akron, before we began the workday. I would carry cylinder blocks, clean up his workspace and make cement for him. That was, by far, the hardest work I ever experienced in my lifetime. He paid me $80 for every day that I worked with him. He taught me how to earn an honest day's wages.

My father's mother, Mary James Sharpe, was another amazing role model in my life. She was born in Alabama in 1915. She passed away in 2017 at 102 years of age. I learned so much from her over the years. She was another positive influence who taught me about hard work and even more about black history. My grandmother was born when Woodrow Wilson was president and lived through 18 U.S Presidents during her lifetime, including the first and only black president, Barack Obama. My grandmother told me stories about how intense the segregation was for blacks in Alabama. She told me about white people yelling derogatory words and throwing things at them as they walked to school.

She spoke of how the color of your skin could cost you your life, just for trying to get a quality education. Today, a quality education is free and available for all youth. Yet, we are unable to get most of our kids to attend school or put their best foot forward to succeed.

The stories she shared about her lifetime were some of the most amazing tales I've ever had the pleasure of hearing. The stories I read in my history books were actual events that my grandmother experienced. For example, the 1st and 2nd Great Migration, the civil rights movement, Brown v. Board of Education, the death of Emmett Till, the Montgomery Bus Boycott, the beginning and the end of Dr. Martin Luther King Jr. and so much more. Through all the trials and tribulations, and the racial equalities that she endured, she still pursued her education and graduated from college.

She was a true family treasure.

Mr. H

I preach that we are a product of our decisions and not our environments, but for a lot of kids, it's not an easy task to separate decisions and environments at such a young age, especially when nobody is showing them the difference between them. During my early years, I was lucky to meet a man by the name of Mr. H who worked at Joy Park Recreation Center. He always treated me with respect and taught me about the importance of character. I don't really know why I chose to listen to him, but I'm glad that I did. He was the positive male role model that I needed and was a tremendous influence on my life. Some kids aren't lucky enough to have that growing up.

I started going to Joy Park Rec when I was six and continued into high school. It was a safe, neutral place where kids could be normal kids. You couldn't go in there repping gang colors or anything like that. I really appreciated that place because it was safe. We'd play basketball, pool, board games and just be kids.

Although the rec was a safe haven, outside of those doors was still toxic. The rec was in the hood and we'd see gang bangers sitting across the street, wearing The Bloods' red colors. Sometimes when the rec center closed, I'd have to sit and hide from the gangs while I waited for my mom to pick me up.

Mr. H ran the Joy Park Recreation Center as the Director. He took responsibility for every kid in that place. It's funny because I feel the same way today about the kids in the community. Mr. H always spoke to us about the importance of having a good moral character. "At the end of the day," he told us, "all that people are going to know you by is your character."

I didn't understand it at first, but then it began to make sense. Your character is everything. It doesn't matter how much money you have or don't have. It's your character that makes you who you are. It's developing your character that makes you into who you want to be. It's what people know and remember you by. I still live by that lesson today and share it with other children. Having good character will take you a long way in life.

While I was shooting my documentary, I ran into Mr. H for the first time in a while. I hugged him tightly and told him, "Mr. H, you don't even realize how much you impacted me. I'm so thankful for everything you instilled in me as a young man."

"Wow," he replied, "I had no idea I helped you like that."

"Yeah," I told him, "and now I take those things you taught me and carry them with me. I teach the same lessons to every kid I meet."

Mr. H is no longer working at Joy Park Rec, but he still works with kids to this day. I'm blessed to take what he taught me and pay it forward. Today, I feel like I'm being Mr. H for the kids I encounter in my life.

Mr. H, my mom and my grandparents all played an instrumental role in my development and helped me get to where I am today. I had some angels looking out for me when I was young.

But don't be mistaken, this story has monsters, too.

CHAPTER 3

FIRST ASSAULT

The Babysitter

There's another story from my childhood that took me quite some time to talk about. I'm blessed that I'm able to share it today and help others who have similar experiences. When I was about five years old, I was sexually assaulted by my babysitter.

One of my mom's best friends had a daughter who babysat me when my parents went bowling or out to have a night for themselves. My mom's friend lived right across the driveway from us and her daughter was about 13 at the time. Before my mom and dad would leave, I would take a bath and get into my pajamas. Then I would go watch TV or play in my room.

The babysitter would come over and watch me. When my parents would leave, she would tell me to take a bath.

"I already took a bath," I told her.

"But now you can put all your toys in there and stuff," she replied. "Um... okay," I said.

She would touch me while I was taking a bath. Even at five years old, I thought it all felt a bit strange, but I didn't think too much about it. When she put me to bed, she would take her clothes off, lay in the bed with me and put me on top of her. She would then put me inside of her.

I vividly remember saying, "I feel like I have to pee." "Go ahead and pee," she said. *Inside of her.*

I've never been able to comprehend if I was feeling the sensation of ejaculating. Of course, I was only five, so I don't think I even had anything in the pipes back then. I'm not sure if it's even possible, but I do remember feeling like I had to pee when I was inside of her.

This all happened more than once. Even in high school, after we moved, we would go over to the babysitter's house.

"Do we really have to go over there?" I asked my mom. But I never told her why I didn't want to go.

The babysitter was a heavy-set girl who had me completely on edge while I was in her presence. She would look at me menacingly and try to get me into her room.

At the time that I was molested and throughout my childhood, part of me thought that she cared about me and was trying to show me love. I kind of felt like that was love, like she was teaching me grown-up love. But at the same time, I was hearing in school that this was wrong and unacceptable behavior. In school, we were taught not to let adults touch us like that. But I still kind of viewed her as a kid. It was like the rules didn't apply, but they did a little bit. It was a tricky and confusing time for me, as well as humiliating.

And I couldn't tell anybody.

Breaking the Silence

Years later, my dad and I were out on one of our many fishing trips on our boat when I said, "Do you remember that babysitter who used to watch us kids? Do you know she used to sexually molest me?"

"What?" He asked, "How old were you?"

"I was like four or five," I said. "When you and mom used to go out."

He chuckled, "What? You were getting booty when you were five?" At first, he treated it like a joke.

"Did you just hear what I said?" I asked him. Then it sunk in. "Oh wow," he said.

My father didn't realize that I was being serious at the time. I think he was a bit upset, because he was very quiet for the remainder of the fishing trip. I'm not sure he knew how to handle the news.

A few years later, I was at an event in a school when I heard someone else talking about being sexually assaulted. I saw the look on her face, and it drew me back to when I was young. As I listened to her talk about it, I felt the need to share what happened to me. I felt like a weight had been lifted off me.

Everybody looked at me – this big dude – talking about this stuff. Inside, I had this feeling that somebody there probably needed to hear that. And they did. Afterwards, someone approached me and said, "I was sexually assaulted, too."

Something magical happened that night.

A Mother's Love
Because of my dad's reaction and the fact that this was one of her closest friend's daughters, I didn't tell my mom back then. It wasn't until a year or two ago that I finally told her.

I knew that my mom wouldn't be here forever and I wanted her to know what happened. I wanted to trust her with this truth and talk to her about it. The day that I told her, we were in my office at the foundation and she was cleaning up as usual.

"Mom, whatever happened to your old friend?" I asked. "Is she alive or do you know what happened to her?"

"I think she died," she said, "Why?" "I have to tell you something," I said.

She sensed that this was serious and stopped cleaning. "Okay, what's up?"

"Mom," I said, "remember when you and dad used to go out and have her daughter babysit me? Yeah, well she used to touch me."

"What do you mean *touch you?*" she asked.

"She used to have sex with me," I said, "and I was only four or five." A horrified look came across her face.

"Oh my God!" she said. "Why didn't you tell me?"

At that moment I just kind of paused. I don't know why I never told my mom, but I think it was because this was her best friend's daughter. I didn't want anyone to get in trouble. It was a hard place for a kid, but when I told her that day, the largest weight was finally lifted off. This was a new type of ease and freedom. My mom hugged me and told me how sorry she was.

My mom did some research and found that her friend had passed away. I told my mom about the time I saw her daughter at a peewee football game in Akron. When I saw her, this childlike scaredness came over me. Me. This big ex-football player, police officer, confident grown-ass man. But at that moment, I was a scared little boy. I had goosebumps and my hair stood up. I just drifted away from the field with my back to her, fading out so I wouldn't have to address it or make contact with her.

That's what trauma does, I think. Takes you back to a place you don't want to be. It makes you regress instead of progress. I can say that talking about it allowed me to let it go and move forward. But it did cause some issues growing up. For years after that happened, the slightest sensation from the air would make me aroused and I could never understand why. I understand that every guy gets aroused when they wake up. It's just "man law," but this was something quite different. It was little things, like drying off with a towel. Stuff would cause me to be aroused with no forewarning. It wasn't like I was staring at older women in bras in a JC

Penney's catalog. It wasn't anything like that. I would get completely aroused out of nowhere. And every single time, I'd feel ashamed.

It took a long time to muster up the courage to peek behind the wall I had put up. The mind can be a very complex thing. All that time I was aware of it, but I was not addressing it. I couldn't comprehend why I was getting aroused like that.

It was like I was drinking Viagra water. Now, I'm like, *shoot, I am going to need those days when I'm 70 and they all were wasted.*

I'm joking about this now as some type of traumatic defense mechanism, but I grew very protective of my kids and the kids in the community. Nothing like this should ever happen to a kid. Without a doubt, being molested was a negative experience, but it also played a part in what I do today – protect kids against anything like that, to the fullest extent.

When I got the building for the foundation, the very first thing I did was put up cameras. I told the board, "No kid will walk through this door until we get cameras in here."

I don't want anything to happen to these kids.

Reflections

This terrible part of my childhood would make me stronger in life, but carrying this secret for so long was emotionally draining. For so many years, I was forced to live with a total feeling of disgust, betrayal and shame. How could someone do this to someone's child? Yes, she was a child herself, but there is a big difference between a 13-year-old and a 5-year-old. Thinking back, I sometimes wonder if she was molested, as well. Maybe she thought this was a normal behavior.

I don't think there was much my parents could have done to prevent what happened back then. I don't know that they could've asked the right questions that would get the truth out of me. We had so many other burdens going on that I didn't want to burden my mom with something like that. I watched my mom struggle a lot, getting the lights cut off and getting very little government assistance. I didn't want to bother her with anything else.

All I can say is... any opportunity you get to bond and hang out with your kids, take it. Ask them if everything is alright and if anything is going on that they feel uncomfortable about. What issues are they having? Just ask questions and listen to them. Hear them.

Gain that trust. Keep it and protect it, so when you say, "You can tell me anything," they will want to. You should be their rock and sounding board. My kids are older now, but I still make time to listen. I pull them aside and say, "Hey, let's go to lunch" or "Let's go see a movie."

Take time to be your child's parent.

CHAPTER 4

PATHWAYS

Baller

Luckily, life on the streets never became a viable option for me, which allowed me to put more focus into sports. When I was a sophomore, my mom lost the house and moved us to a better neighborhood where there wasn't as much violence. We moved from the projects to Goodyear Heights. Not being able to pay the bills was a blessing in disguise.

There was a lot less crime in the Heights. It was freedom. Without the constant stress of just staying alive, I was able to put more focus on positive outlets. I started to stand out on the football field. Even though I was a really good athlete and received many awards around the city, county and state, I was not the best athlete in my neighborhood. There were guys who ran circles around me with the talent they had. The difference between them and me was that I set out to achieve my dream and avoided the negative things that could have derailed me. So many dudes in my neighborhood wanted to be superstar athletes, but they wouldn't leave the street life to achieve that dream.

I, on the other hand, wanted to get as far away from home as possible. I knew that if I stayed around Akron, there was a chance that I would get sucked into the life I knew as a child. Throughout my childhood, I kept repeating a mantra in the back of my mind.

Just try not to get in trouble.

I stayed focused, getting recruited to play football by almost every school in the country. I flew to a few different schools for recruiting visits, which was the first time I'd ever been on a plane. Before football, flying was a luxury I could never afford. Football gave me the opportunity to see places that I would have never seen otherwise. I traveled to these different schools and realized that they were not like home. They were safe places to roam, study and excel. Even though I'd been an Ohio State fan all my life, it wasn't in my best interest to stay so close to home. So instead, I chose to play football at the University of Kansas.

So many people knock the sport of football, but it gave me the motivation to chase after a dream and removed me from a potential nightmare of being dead or incarcerated. It gave me the chance to see Hawaii, a trip my mom would have loved to take us children on, but she could never afford it.

Intro to Division I

Many people told me that, coming out of a small school like Akron's East High, I would never play at a big school like the University of Kansas. They told me that I should go to a small Division II school. Hearing people say those things made me so angry, but I turned their doubts and my anger into motivation. I arrived in Kansas in 1994, feeling good and confident about myself and my ability to play at the Division I level.

My freshman year at the University of Kansas, #98.

All the new freshmen reported to camp a few days earlier than the older players and I did really well playing linebacker, a position I was not accustomed to. At the conclusion of freshman camp, the coaches were telling me how great I did. I was getting a lot of attention from coaches and players alike. My confidence was at an all-time high.

I can do this. I can play at this level.

A few days later, the upperclassmen reported to camp. These guys were much bigger, faster and stronger than the freshmen I'd been competing against for the last few days. They got all the attention and all the reps. I became a spectator, watching them from the sidelines. Realizing that I had no chance of playing right away, my all-time high feeling went to an all-time low. I was hurt, frustrated, angry and alone, conceding to those who had told me that I couldn't play at this level of competition. I was so distraught about the situation that I called my mom, asking her to call the coaches at Ohio State and a few other schools. I was ready to transfer immediately. She refused. Instead, she told me to hang in there and everything would get better when the time is right. Like always, she was right. As it turned out, the team needed a pass rusher on our scout team. I jumped at the opportunity and earned the spot, never looking back. That opportunity allowed me to be one of the five true freshmen to play that season.

During that first season, I regained my confidence and continued to progress in my new role. My dreams of playing in the NFL seemed attainable. But the universe had other plans for me.

Blow Out
On the very first play of my sophomore year, I blew out my knee. The doctor had to perform reconstructive knee surgery and reattach almost everything in my left knee. For the next two months, my leg was locked at a 45° angle so everything

would heal correctly. The doctors told me that my football career was probably over.

I wouldn't accept that. Again, someone was telling that I couldn't do something. And again, I used it as fuel. I had to prove them wrong. This was definitely one of the biggest challenges I would ever face in life.

Physical therapy broke me down physically, mentally and emotionally. The next season, I made it back on the field to prove the doubters wrong, but I was certainly not the same player I once was. I was so frustrated that I couldn't do the things I once did on the field, but I was proud of myself for achieving this goal. The whole time I was dealing with this frustration on the field, I was also dating a girl back in Ohio.

My girlfriend at the time (who would go on to become my wife... and then my ex-wife) had a four-year-old daughter, Imari, from a previous relationship. I fell in love with Imari the moment I laid eyes on her. Her father was murdered in a senseless act of violence when she was just two years old. Ironically, his homicide took place in the exact same zone where I would start community policing years later. I never knew her dad, but I made a promise to him to always love her and protect her for the rest of my life. Imari is 26 years old now and the promise I made to her deceased father is something that I continue to hold dearly in my heart to this day.

A New Position
We were playing The University of Cincinnati at their home field when my girlfriend went into labor. After the football game, I flew back to Kansas and immediately flew to Ohio to see my daughter Armani enter the world.

I decided to end my college career and returned home to help raise my first child. Meanwhile, I did a workout with the Miami Dolphins and tried out for the Browns when they returned to Cleveland in 1999 (God knows they needed all the help they could get back then), but it never happened for me. During all of this, I was selling vacuum cleaners to provide for my new family. Our small family doubled with the addition of my daughters Trysten and Alexa, along with my two sons LaMar Jr. and Desmond. I had to sell a lot of vacuum cleaners! Can you imagine someone my size selling vacuum cleaners, door-to-door?

There I was – this huge 6'6", 255 lb. dude, selling vacuum cleaners as I tried out for the NFL.

I was all decked out in a fancy suit, carrying this big box with me, going door to door like, "Hey, I'm just here to show you something."

I wasn't a bad salesman and actually sold a lot of vacuum cleaners. Or maybe my customers were just intimidated by my stature and too afraid to say no to me. It was a fun job, but it required a lot of travel. I had to confirm appointments with clients, and some would act like they weren't home, even when I could see them moving around in the house. It was a weird job for me.

Correction!

After selling vacuum cleaners, I worked as a corrections officer at Faircrest Detention Center. I started working with the kids there, watching them come in for everything from unruly conduct to murder. In that building, we had every type of trouble imaginable in the city of Canton. The kids in that place could smell fear. Whether it came from the other juveniles or the staff, they could sense it. I was a large presence in the jail, but some of the kids that came in were even bigger than me. It was rough. In fact, it was so rough that other corrections officers would come in on their first day, leave their keys on the counter, walk out and never come back.

I developed a great relationship with most of the kids while they were incarcerated, but many of them could turn on you or their fellow inmates in an instant. One day, things would be great and the next day, I would find myself physically restraining someone for going completely off the handle. You never knew what to expect from those kids, but one thing was certain – you could never let your guard down. Some guys got beat up by the kids and I was put in positions where I had to physically restrain some kids. But I always felt that they respected me.

Even after roughing a kid up, I'd take advantage of the opportunity to sit them down and explain, "Hey, listen, you're not on the streets, okay? In here, you lost your freedom. Now, it's my job to tell you what to do and how to act. Now, let's talk about you and why you're here."

Once you've opened that door, you can start developing a real connection.

I took every opportunity I could get to steer those young men in the right direction. I ran the physical training program at the detention center. Pretty soon, every kid wanted to be a front row leader of the exercises. It made them feel a sense of pride to earn one of those spots. I made an impact there. I even had rival gang members who were beefing with one another on the streets, coexisting in the same room together (which was completely against detention center rules).

When it was visitation time, most of the visitors were mothers. It became clear that many of these young men needed a father figure.

I didn't see those boys as troublemakers, I only saw myself in them. I could've become a product of my environment, but I decided not to. Some kids don't understand how to avoid that. For so many of them, even if they did well inside the detention center, after they were released, many of them would just go right back into their old environments and situations. And the next thing you know, they're right back in jail full of pain and regret. I could see that they were hurting, because they wouldn't look at me when they returned to the center.

On the way to the detention center, they'd tell the escorting police officers, "Mr. Sharpe is going to be so mad at me" or "Mr. Sharpe is going to be so disappointed."

Some of the police officers, who brought the kids in, came to me and said,

"I don't know what you're doing to these kids, but they respect you and talk highly of you. You need to take the police test."

On the Fence
I still had this real distrust with the police growing up. So, for them to ask me to take the test was like... *fool, you crazy.* Where I came from, we do not join that team. It's not happening. Not even an option.

My loyalty to my hood and my pride were hindering me from wanting to become a police officer. I felt like my neighborhood would disown me. On the flip side, I had a family to take care of and I knew this would be a wise career move to make that happen. I didn't want my children to face the struggles I did growing up. Once I put it in that perspective, it was a no-brainer to pursue a law enforcement career to improve my financial situation and really become a protector for my children.

Even though I didn't exactly want to be a cop, I started thinking, *Man, I'm making $8 an hour at this youth detention center.* At that time, I was also working a few days a week at SRCCC, a drug and alcohol treatment facility, where adults were sentenced for treatment instead of going to prison. It is similar to a halfway house. When I started thinking about the salary of a police officer, making $50,000 to $100,000 a year, I was like, "Where do I sign up?"

Still uncertain, I signed up for the test, which I didn't think I could pass. They gave us a booklet to study, which I didn't study. I just kind of stared at it, saying to myself, *I absolutely do not want to be a police officer.*

The day before the test, I still didn't want to take it. But then I looked at my situation and my bank account. *I'd better go take this test.* I opened the pamphlet and read it a little bit, but I kept getting these signs that this wasn't meant to be. The day I was supposed to take the test, we were supposed to show up with our IDs. That day, I lost my ID. Again, I told myself this wasn't meant to be.

It was a struggle within myself and my beliefs.

Regardless of the test, I still needed my license to drive anywhere. There was still some time before testing began, so I went to the BMV to get a new license. I knew I'd be standing in line at the BMV for a very long time and wouldn't be able to make it in time for the test. I made peace with that. But when I walked into the BMV, I immediately got called for my turn. There was still time.

I sat in my car and, literally, convinced myself to take the police test. I showed up, passed the test, completed a lengthy process and ended up getting hired as a police officer. It was unbelievable.

If I would have let my circumstances or fear dictate my life, who knows what I'd be doing today. That decision led to this amazing path that I'm on right now. As I write this story, I have been a police officer with the City of Canton Police Department for 18 years. Being on the force has allowed me to connect with our youth and our community. It also paved the way for my greatest accomplishments in life: my wife, my children and my foundation.

*Me and the former police chief, Chief Wyatt,
on the day I swore in as an officer.*

CHAPTER 5

OFFICER SHARPE

Evolution of Authority

When I was in the 5th and 6th grade, I was a school crossing guard for my school, Robinson Elementary. When they gave me my crossing pole, safety belt and badge, I remember feeling very proud and honored. At an early age, I was responsible for the safety of the students at my school. I took my role seriously and climbed up the ranks really fast, going from Sergeant to Captain in no time at all. I was also one of the few crossing guards in the state to earn a trip to Cedar Point. The pride I felt wearing that crossing guard badge is the same pride I feel wearing this police badge today.

When I first started out as a police officer, I would ride in my cruiser and wave at people. In return, kids would literally flip me off. I'd think to myself, *where did you learn that?* But back when I was growing up, I had learned that same mentality from some of my friends.

It really was "F*@k the police."

But when you turn your nose up at a kid who disrespects you, it doesn't help anyone. You don't know what traumatic events that kid has experienced in his/her life. Many people turn their back on certain kids before they get to know them.

> *Some of these kids just want some attention;*
> *they just want to know that someone cares about them.*

That's all it is. These kids just need to know there is someone rooting for them and pushing them to do better. I know a lot of adults who need the same thing. Serena Williams, Tiger Woods and every other superstar athlete needs encouragement, just like we all do. Don't you think that someone a fraction of your age could use a little encouragement? Of course they could. Give them some encouragement.

During my first few years with the department, I felt like I was established as a person and comfortable with my moral character. As a police officer, though, I knew I had room to grow. I learned a lot by watching good officers that I worked with every day. Although I may not have said it out loud, I made a conscious choice to say, "I like what you're doing as a police officer and I'm going to add some of those things into my own repertoire."

And so, I took what I was learning from other officers and incorporated all of it into who I was as a police officer. In those early days, one of my biggest positive influencers was Officer Baskerville, who was my partner for nine years. He was absolutely amazing with the people in the community. Every call we went on, everyone seemed to know Officer Baskerville, and he had a great relationship with them. I really admired him for that. From the moment I joined the force, he has been like a big brother to me. I am so grateful for the many officers I've worked with over the years, who have taught me so much. I often tell people who make comments like "I wish there were more officers like you," that I work with a lot of amazing officers who I feel are better than me. They just aren't on social media and getting the word out like I am.

Discrimination
I haven't had a perfect experience in this role, but I learn from every encounter, good or bad. I've been a victim of discrimination on a few different occasions in this job. Working in a Canton community that was similar to the one I grew up in, I would hear a lot of people in the black community call me an "Uncle Tom," a "sellout," or say that I'm working for "the master." That really hurt me, especially when I was only there to make the community safe. I was, and still am, only trying to remove the bad elements of the

community and make it a safer place where kids can go outside and play freely.

I remember one particular call when my partner and I responded to a white couple who had a problem with their black neighbor. The couple proceeded to tell us that they would prefer other (non-black) officers to help them with this call. We informed them that we were just as qualified as any other officers. They did not want to talk to us at all and were very adamant about us sending other officers to help them. We ended up leaving and informed our dispatchers that if they called back again, to send us again. It just didn't make sense to us.

During this time, the crack epidemic was booming. When you're on this job long enough, you see the swings of different drugs taking over. Crack --> meth

--> heroin is the way it went down in my area. In the zone I was working, you had to be careful. Users and dealers were putting crack in places where things shouldn't go. As officers, we also had to be careful because there was a lot of hepatitis going around and people would carry syringes everywhere. We had to be careful when we were patting somebody down because we could get poked by a syringe. That was a big fear for me.

Not only was I battling the pressures of the neighborhoods I worked in, but I was also dealing with problems within my own department with one of my supervisors. One day, a supervisor stopped me while I was working and said to me, "Do you think this office is an f'ing walkthrough boy?"

I looked at him and said, "What did you just say to me?" "You f'ing heard me, boy," he replied.

I walked up on him, ready to deliver a beat down. At that point, I could care less about his rank or losing my job. My own dad didn't even talk to me like that and I damn sure wasn't going to let anyone else talk to me like that. I was ready for battle, but luckily, the officer working at the report desk jumped out of his chair and grabbed me. If it wasn't for him, I would have easily lost my job that night. I was so angry that I walked out of work that evening. Having pressures from the inside and the outside had me contemplating if I could continue doing this job. Thankfully, I have never been a quitter and I sure wasn't going to let anyone run me off.

Especially when there was so much bad stuff going on in the streets.

Homicide
I've been on numerous calls for shootings and homicides, but I'll never forget my first homicide call. A gentleman was shot in the head, lying dead on the sidewalk. I remember looking at him and almost throwing up. I was queasy, to say the least.

Right or wrong, this job changes you. It just desensitizes you. I eventually reached a point where we would get homicide calls and I'd be getting out of the car, still eating. Standing over a victim and gathering evidence, while I'm munching down on a Snickers bar, not queasy at all. Unfortunately, you get used to it. It's sad that you get hardened like that as a police officer, but when you see so much of it, that's what happens.

Sexual Assault
Being a parent and being molested myself, one of the worst things I've ever seen was on a molestation call. A lady's boyfriend had been raping her young son. I went to the hospital to do the report and examination, and this little boy was laying on a table – with his rectum wide open. I was so angry and sad at the same time. Then all I could feel was uncontrollable rage. All I wanted to do was hurt the man who did this. I remember sitting there across from him and staring him down. He was just acting all cocky with no remorse, saying things like, "Ya'll ain't got nothing on me."

The natural human instinct is to want to pummel this man. Attack him and hurt him. How the hell could you do that to a child? But the thing is, you can't take this job if you can't control that instinct or you'll end up in prison just like this man. I had to learn to control my emotions on this job, really quick, and trust in the justice system.

House Fire

I'll never forget this call that came in on Christmas Eve. A house fire broke out and we got dispatched. This was during a time when fire departments were being shut down and rotated, so the closest fire department to this area was closed. My partner and I were working midnights. I was sitting in the passenger seat when the dispatcher came on the radio.

"There is a fire truck in route, but if you guys can head there, there is a house on fire."

We took off and arrived on the scene, which was one street over from my house at the time. What we later discovered is that the parents went out for the night and left real candles on their Christmas tree. The tree caught on fire and sent the house up in flames. We were told earlier that there were possibly five kids in this house. At this time, I had five kids at home. It got real, real fast. We pulled up and I saw the fire upstairs.

I jumped out of the cruiser before it we even put it in park. Another car was on the scene in front of the house, so I ran to the back door. I booted the door, but it didn't open. I booted it again. This time it swung open and the roof was falling everywhere. It was apparent that I couldn't enter that way, so I ran to the side of the house and jumped on a parked car in the driveway to call to the kids to the window. All I could see was fire.

The house was burning rapidly and none of the kids were coming to the window.

Meanwhile, the fire department had arrived and were attempting to put the fire out. When I came around front, they were carrying the kids out, one by one. Tears were in my eyes, but I was still trying to hold it together and do my job as the firemen did theirs.

When we were no longer needed at the scene, we sped to the hospital. There's a very distinct smell when a fire like that gets embedded in your clothes. All I could smell was smoke. We rushed in the hospital and saw all five kids curled up, their flesh peeled from their bodies.

They were all dead.

I went back to the cruiser and couldn't stop crying. After that call, I went home on Christmas Day morning with this tragedy on my mind and this gratefulness in my heart to be able to be in the presence of my kids. I kissed my kids and told them I loved them, still smelling the fire in my clothes. That was one of the worst nights of my life.

One of the scariest nights of my life, though, was still yet to come.

The Night My Daughter Got Shot
One night, a young man named Jalen, who was pretty well-known in the Canton area, got shot in the head and died. Months later, we would find out that it was his childhood friend who killed him over some money Jalen owed him. At the location where he died three days earlier, a memorial was held in his honor. Both of my daughters, Alexa and Armani, knew Jalen and decided to go to his memorial to pay their respects. They were hanging out with other young adults, sitting on the porch and having a cookout.

A car came by and stopped, idling, near the house. My daughter later told me that she felt like something wasn't right. Before anyone could make sense of the suspicious vehicle, shots rang out. Kids started jumping over the porch, trying to hide and looking for cover.

It was automatic gunfire from an AK-47.

During the shooting, one of the rounds hit something and exploded, sending five pieces of shrapnel into my daughter's thigh. When my daughter called me, I was in the shower. My wife handed me the phone, saying that my daughter needed me and it was an emergency. The first thing she said was "Dad, don't be mad, but I was shot in the leg and I need you to come to the hospital." I jumped out of the shower, still soap-covered, and flew to the hospital.

Mind you, Armani was one of my older kids who had been born when I was still learning how to be a good parent. She expected anger, and rightfully so.

Even though I was thankful that my daughter was alive, I was still angry. The protector part of me just wanted to go hurt somebody. I wanted to hunt down the city and find out who did this. *Who shoots a crowd of people?*

In the Honor Guard.

Thankfully, she ended up having surgery to remove the shrapnel and is fine today.

Never in a million years would I – Mr. Community Man, Officer Sharpe – dream I would be put in a situation where one of my children was shot. If somebody would've asked me if I ever thought something like that could happen to me, I would've said they were nuts.

It was a learning experience as a police officer, a father and a human. Rather than focusing on my anger, thanks to years of service and lots of lessons in love and compassion, my thought process was this: if I could've reached whoever shot my daughter and helped him first, maybe this wouldn't have happened. Or, if somebody in the community would have reached out to this young man to keep him on a straight path, maybe this type of thing wouldn't have happened. You feel me?

> *I don't want to look down and see another kid shot –*
> *a kid I know or a kid I could've saved.*

We all have a responsibility to teach others and help them get on a better path. That's exactly what the power of community policing will accomplish.

CHAPTER 6

COMMUNITY POLICING

A Storm in the Streets

For years, we've been witnessing this epidemic across the country; more and more backlash between the police and the community. Distrust. Anger. Fear. There have been times when I have been afraid for my life. Officers are going on calls and getting shot. Unarmed black men are being killed by police. Every time you turn on the news, it is the first story in the headlines. These stories just add to the distrust between the police and civilians.

Imagine being a police officer and a black man at the same time? While some can only imagine, I have lived it.

In 2013, I was off-duty, traveling home from a local water park with my kids when I was stopped by a police agency adjacent to my local police department. I was traveling on the highway in my H3 Hummer that I had purchased ten days prior. My kids were sound asleep in the passenger and back seats. I had my driver side window rolled down and my arm resting on the door. I passed a police cruiser sitting in the median with no concern. I wasn't breaking any laws - I was neither speeding nor going too slow. About a half mile down the road, the cruiser pulled me over.

When the officer approached my vehicle, he informed me that he was stopping me because I had fictitious plates and that my plates came back to a Ford Expedition. As a police officer, I completely understood his reasoning and had no problem with the stop at all. I informed him that I just purchased this vehicle and I did, in fact, transfer my plates from my old vehicle to my current vehicle. He asked to see my registration and I immediately informed him that I was a police officer and had my duty weapon and badge in my middle console. The officer took a half step back and wrapped his hands around his holstered firearm as he asked to see my credentials. After seeing this motion, I put my hands in the air and informed him that I would not reach for anything. I told him that I would like it if he confirmed that I am a police officer with his dispatchers before I made any more movements.

I was honestly afraid that this officer was going to shoot me with my kids sitting right beside me in my car. I was beyond angry. This police officer, who may have had three or four years on the job, proceeded to educate me on the BMV laws pertaining to the transfer of plates and told me that I should know better. But he had no clue about the laws of transferring plates in the State of Ohio. My first instinct was to go off on him. Instead, I contacted my supervisor and he directed me to file a formal complaint on the officer.

This incident took me back to a place of distrust with the police and the worst part about it is, I *am* the police.

Taking the Leap

Even though I knew something needed to be done to mend the relationship between police and community residents, I didn't seem to know how to do my part to help. The only way I knew to get started was to just do everything I could to inspire change.

There's been more and more police departments that ask me to come in and talk about community policing. Community policing revolves around the concept that, together, officers and residents can build proactive problem-solv- ing solutions for crime and violence. Getting started in community policing is a simple enough concept. You, the police officer, just have to get out of your cruiser! Many officers don't take the time to get out and talk to people. They want to maintain a removed, tough guy image or something, which only hurts them and the community they are serving.

When I first came on the job, we had a community policing department. It consisted of officers on bicycles and a walking beat. When it was time for budget cuts, there was no 'community' anything. When we lost the D.A.R.E. programs, everything went a bit sideways. All of a sudden, there was nobody telling kids to stay off drugs or to not bully one another. We lost our way a little bit and, as a community, we started to notice it. We started seeing the rise in tension between the community and police. We started to feel it. That's when community policing started making its way back into more departments.

It's a critical piece of the puzzle that every police department needs. Without it, a lot of other problems arise and continue to compound.

I get out of my cruiser to ask people in the community how they are doing and make sure everything is okay. You're building a relationship with the community and working to change a stigma that doesn't have to exist. Looking back on my childhood, I now do what I wanted the officers in my old neighborhood to do – get out and get to know me! The tiny act of getting out of my cruiser has been instrumental in my success as a police officer.

Community Policing is Parties and BBQs...
A lot of people in the community have invited me to birthday parties, cookouts, weddings, even bar mitzvahs! Before I started getting out of my cruiser, and interacting with the people within it, these types of invites were not happening.

I remember the first time I got out of my cruiser and smelled an amazing BBQ party in the neighborhood. I'll admit, I was hungry, but I also wanted to show the people in my community that I was human. I got out of my cruiser and the music stopped. It was so quiet that you could've heard a churchmouse fart. It's like in those movies where someone walks into the party and the DJ scratches the record into complete silence. All eyes were on me.

I'm like, "Hey, I'm just coming over to see how everyone's doing. Nobody is in trouble. Everybody alright? What y'all cooking over here? Some smack your mama ribs? (Tucking a napkin in my collar as a bib). Someone send me a plate and I'll be the judge of that."

I played a game of cards with them and you could see everyone taken aback. Like, *this is a human dude right here.*

... But It's Much More

If you're a police officer, and not in tune with your community, you're basically here to get a paycheck and go home. And that's unacceptable in this job. You must love what you do and love the community you're serving. Luckily, I really do love both. When I decided to become a police officer, it was to earn a better living, but it turned out it also made me a better person.

When you get involved in the community, you start to know and understand the people in it, as opposed to simply meeting your arrest quotas. You get to learn who the people are and understand their families. You get to learn how you can really help them by giving them what they need or what can help them.

The actions of a bad officer can cost me my life.

Community policing needs to be more supported in this country. I believe it's trending that way, but there are certainly bad police officers out there who give the rest of us a bad rap.

Here I am a pillar of the community, who is trying to help the world. And yet, somebody in another part of the world can do something that can cost me my life, even though it has nothing to do with me. Police officers need to be aware that they are a part of a larger team. Any negative actions or attitudes of one teammate in one city could cost another officer his/her life in another.

I work with a lot of amazing officers in my police department, guys and gals who would give the shirt off their backs to help someone in need. It is sad that when they have to arrest someone, they are labeled as bad officers. They are doing their job and upholding the laws that are in place to keep the world safe. In addition to making arrests when laws have been broken, we need those officers out there being proactive and deterring crime. It's a balance that every department should have.

Like everything else in life, there is no one-size-fits-all solution. We swore and signed on the dotted line to serve and protect, and community policing is a way to do that on a much deeper, intimate level. It feels good for us as officers, but it feels even better for those who know you're there for them and truly care about them.

When you learn who people are and their family dynamics, you can inspire a much greater level of change. When you take the time to learn about the people their families, grandparents, parents and kids – that stuff goes a long way. So, when you catch someone doing something wrong (or about to do something wrong), it's a much better angle to come in and correct them by saying, "Hey listen, if I can help you, I'll help you. You need to learn from this situation and grow. But I can't always help you, especially if it will cost me my job. I have to do what I have to do, and you have to respect that."

You'd be surprised what you can accomplish with this approach.

What I hear is, "I respect that. If I'm doing something wrong, I understand you have to do your job."

Good! We're still friends.

During my 18 years on the force, I've made hundreds of arrests. Even though

I have a job to do, I've never disrespected anyone who I took to jail, no matter what the crime. What if that was your mom, dad, brother, sister or your child? I've always tried to talk to them and send some positive energy their way in hopes that they do not make the same bad decision again. Many people I've arrested have thanked me for being kind and not treating them as anything less than human. People make mistakes and, unfortunately, there are consequences for their actions. But the truth is that some people don't have a voice of reason or anyone to give them positive advice in their lives. Not every person I've arrested was willing to talk to me, but I still tried. And I've always wished them the best in their future.

Community policing is about respecting people. In turn, they'll respect you and your position of authority.

Show Some Respect!

I go to different police academies and speak to different groups and officers who may be set in their ways. I tell them all the same thing, that this job can make you or break you.

I've spent my entire career working in high crime areas, while still treating people with respect. If you're going around as one of those officers who thinks they can disrespect everybody just because they have a badge, there are some hard dudes out there who *will* put you down. Period. They'll get you, on or off duty. To a small percentage of the population, that badge means nothing. So, as an officer, please do not go around thinking you're super tough and picking on everybody. If you're going around like that and you disrespect the wrong person, someday you might find yourself in a situation where your attitude comes back to bite you.

If you treat people with respect, you'll get respect.

Hypothetically, let's say you get jumped on the street and the person you disrespected is walking by. It's likely that person will say, "Oh, that's the officer who thought they were tough and disrespected everyone. I hope they kick that officer's butt."

That person is going to keep on walking by, wishing you the worst.

But guess what? If you treated that same person with respect and they walked by, they are much more likely to come to your aid as an ally. They might say,

"That officer treated me like a human and doesn't deserve to die."

Some of these young officers don't understand that. It's the difference they need to see. We are in a position of authority, but it doesn't have to be disrespectful. It is our duty to serve and protect the people in our communities. There's no better way to do that than to do it with respect.

I'm a pretty big dude, standing at 6'6", 275 pounds, and I'm not worried about validating my toughness to anyone. I don't need to prove how tough I am, nor should any officer. If you need to prove your toughness, maybe this job isn't for you. Maybe you should pursue MMA or boxing. Being kind and giving back to the community doesn't make you look weak; it makes you look human. It takes a stronger person to control their emotions, especially in this job.

That badge you're wearing comes with a high level of responsibility.

Respect, compassion and kindness always come back around. I tell young officers to become one with their community. When you do, it makes life so much easier. People will have your back, because they know you're a good person. They will vouch for you.

If you go out there thinking you're Wyatt Earp and want to be this regulator without remorse, that's a good way to end up dead or in prison yourself. The community, in which you serve, will not accept you as a police officer or a person. A lot of people come into this profession thinking they can't die or go to prison because they're cops. You're not invincible. If you're a bad police officer to those who rely on you, you're just feeding a negative community and it will come back to haunt you. Or even worse, it will come back to haunt another innocent officer.

It's only through respect that I've gained the trust of my community. It's the same people I've shown respect to on a daily basis who have helped me build a foundation of positivity for all of us.

PART

II

THE BE A BETTER ME FOUNDATION

CHAPTER 7

PILLARS

It Started with a Dream

I'd always had hopes of creating a non-profit organization to help kids, but what started everything was simple humanity and taking a different approach to what was going on in the neighborhood. I told you that one day when I was on patrol, I waved at a kid and he gave me the finger. Now, I could have been upset and reacted in an aggressive manner, but I didn't. Instead, I got out of my cruiser and talked to him. I offered him some of my lunch that I had packed for myself that day and made a new friend. In turn, that young kid told all his friends I was cool. When I entered that neighborhood a week or so later, all these kids came sprinting from behind their apartments just to see me. I think that's when the "Officer Sharpe phenomenon" began.

After that day, I made it my mission to change the mindset of the people in my community, never thinking that one day I could change the mindset of people around the world. I started putting candy and chips in my cruiser. I'd hand them to kids on the street in between calls. Pretty soon, the community started seeing me as "the candy and chip cop."

For as long as I can remember, I have wanted to help our youth make better decisions that would positively impact their future and, in turn, our world. I wanted to bridge the gap between officers and the community. I had wanted to start this foundation for nearly 20 years before we made it happen. In my early college years, my dream was to make it to the NFL and use that money to build a state-of-the-art youth center. My chances to make it to the NFL eventually faded away, and with them, my dream to open my very own youth center. In my head, I thought that I couldn't have one without the other. Still, I somehow held on the notion that I could make it happen someday. I kept telling myself I'd get to it, but then I'd get caught up with life again – building a family, a home, a career and whatever else came along.

But with all the distrust between police and communities across the country, and seeing so many kids struggling in my very own community, my desire to help couldn't wait any longer.

In the summer of 2016, my wife, fellow board members and I filed the bylaws for the Be A Better Me Foundation. My lifelong dream finally came to fruition.

The Be A Better Me Foundation is a community-based non-profit foundation designed to help empower and encourage youth to see the good in themselves and others. Our goal is to provide hope and influence in the next generation and show them the impact their actions can have on their own lives, families and community.

When we first started Be A Better Me, we were working out of a storage unit. We didn't have the funding to roll out some of the programs we wanted, but we kept pushing. It was a struggle. Regardless of the hardships, I continued my mission to bring unity between the community and the police department. I didn't start this mission for news attention or fame, but suddenly, local radio and news stations were showing up at different events to get the scoop on the Be A Better Me movement. I've never been one to look for any type of attention, but this sudden exposure was boosting support and generating awareness of our cause. It provided the much-needed financial backing that helped the organization grow. It helped us fund and create more programs for the kids in the community.

But it wasn't until May 2018 that the Be A Better Me Foundation reached global awareness. The day that Mike Rowe arrived in Canton, Ohio to forever change the future of this organization.

CHAPTER 8

FAVOR RETURNED

A Homeless Foundation

Late one night, I was working in my home office when I got a call from a film company. Right away, I was skeptical of the entire thing. I was told that this company wanted to feature my story in an upcoming documentary series. After Googling some of the people mentioned without finding much information, it crossed my mind that this group might use the footage for a negative purpose, like to bash police. On top of that, they wanted a background check on me. Something wasn't adding up. I pushed the project aside and went about my business.

My business, at that time, was finding a home for the foundation.

Although the foundation was gaining traction and awareness, we still didn't have the funds to secure a building to house our operations. We were working out of a church that was still providing church services, so we were constantly running around and packing stuff up to move our stuff out of the way. My house and vehicle had become storage units for everything that belonged to the foundation. We couldn't do some of the things we wanted to do and no matter what we had going on, we had to move whenever the church was in use.

Be A Better Me was in desperate need of a home.

The film company contacted me a few more times, but I was laser-focused on finding a permanent place for the foundation. I didn't really know what was going on with this "documentary series" and was about to turn them away once and for all. Right when I was about to back out completely, my board members came to me and said, "LaMar, this is a good thing. You need to do this."

When I say I reluctantly agreed to do the series, I mean I *very* reluctantly agreed.

The wheels were set in motion and I met with the producers the day before we started filming. I was nervous. I was still skeptical and didn't know what to expect. I still had this feeling like someone was trying to set me up. I rode my motorcycle to the meeting and brought my gun with me. I had different scenarios running through my mind, convinced that someone was trying to jeopardize all that I'd been building through the foundation. When I arrived at the meeting, the producers were really nice, but I felt like they were still withholding information. It felt like there were pieces of the puzzle missing.

The producers told me they were going to follow me around for the day and we sat down to create a blueprint of things they wanted to capture on film. On the day of shooting, we met at Carpe Diem, one of my favorite coffee shops in downtown Canton. I hung out with the producers as they wired up the microphone I would wear during the filming. As we sat there talking, I started seeing people with cameras arriving outside. Some of them were moving very fast and all the commotion was weird to me.

One of the producers said, "Okay, Officer Sharpe. We're going to go outside now, and our narrator is going to get on camera and go from there..."

Um. Okay, cool.

Cue Mike Rowe
I walked outside and there were cameras everywhere. *What in the world was going on?* Next, I turned and saw a guy who looked very familiar. I was sure I'd seen this dude on TV or something, but I was drawing a blank.

I smiled nervously. "Man, where do I know you from?" I asked.

He introduced himself as Mike Rowe. But I still couldn't place the name. "I did a little show called *Dirty Jobs*," he said.

"That's it!" I said, "That's where I know you from."

I had watched his show a few weeks before that day, so now I was thinking, *I know I have a dirty job, but is it that dirty?*

We went about our scheduled day. Mike followed me around and we talked a lot. He is a genuinely nice guy – like next-level nice. They filmed me doing some different things and I still wasn't really sure what was going on. After shooting, they dropped me off and I was supposed to meet up with them later to film a little more. This time when I met them, they directed me where I needed to go around the city. I drove around and we talked a bit more. I still had no idea what was yet to come.

The next thing I knew, Mike had me park in downtown Canton. I could see lights and other officers waiting ahead. Now I was really confused. Mike started telling me about his new show, *Returning the Favor*, which had millions of viewers. He told me that they were in search of do-gooders around the country.

"You, my friend, are a do-gooder," Mike said, "and we want to return the favor to you, for everything that you do."

What???

There was a big tarp over one of the buildings on the block. They pulled the tarp down and there was a big old picture of yours truly with the foundation's logo.

This can't actually be happening.

"This is your building for the next two years and it is 100% paid for," he said.

He showed me around the building, and we turned the corner. I was now standing in the main classroom with my entire family, friends, co-workers and so many people in the community who cared about me. Everybody in that room meant something to me.

"Surprise!!!"

I can still name every person there. My emotions took over and I felt the tears roll up in my eyes. Mike began to explain the situation and how they paid the 2-year lease for the foundation's home.

This was insane. I was overcome with joy, but then all I could think about was wishing my dad was here to see it. Before he passed away, he told me how proud he was of my community policing. He told me that big things were going to happen for me. He was a proud father; the one I had wanted my entire life.

Now, all my dreams were coming true and he wasn't there to witness it.

As I was talking to everybody in the room, I was transfixed by the emotions that came with my father's memory. I couldn't stop the tears. I looked over to see my mom and sister crying. Immediately, I became grateful, realizing how happy I was to have my mom, family and friends there.

We had a building. And this day – this building – would change my life forever. Now we could provide our services at a greater level. We could get more creative with the services that we offered. We could do so much more. And to think that I almost skipped out on this documentary because I was dedicated to finding a home for the foundation. What are the chances?

God works in mysterious ways.

After the show aired, I couldn't believe the response from all over the world. I even received messages through social media that required me to hit a translate button just to be able to read them. People are still messaging and emailing me about my story and how it's helping them change their own stories. At the end of the day, all I want to do is inspire people to do better and be better, so we can stop some of the madness in the world. *Returning the Favor*, Mike Rowe and his team helped me do that. They allowed me to inspire many more people from all over the world. They didn't just return the favor. They gave my foundation a shot at becoming a worldwide movement.

They gave hope to a foundation based on hope.

Mike Rowe unveiling The Be A Better Me Foundation's new building.

CHAPTER 9

WHAT WE DO

Changing the Game
The needs of the community are always changing, so our foundation is always adapting and coming up with creative methods to accommodate them. We give free hot meals to those in need. We give them warm clothing, hand warmers, sleeping bags and other cold weather gear. We hold annual Easter egg hunts. We give out hundreds of Halloween costumes. Last year for Christmas, we gave out nearly 1,400 toys to kids in the community.

Each summer, we have an event where we give out thousands of backpacks filled with school supplies to local kids in need. We recently collaborated with another nonprofit organization aspire2day.org and started handing out clear book bags to keep our kids and teachers safe. These book bags allow everybody to see what you're carrying into school. The clear book bags are much more expensive, but at the end of the day, it's about being transparent and keeping people safe. This is an effort I'm trying to push in hopes that every school someday adopts the same standard. It's a safety precaution that is easy and semi-cheap to implement.

We do everything we can to help the kids and the community.

Mentoring Academy
One of the original goals of the foundation was to teach kids how to develop the necessary skills to succeed in the world. And it's happening. Our mentoring academy is the backbone of our foundation. We hold separate eight-week mentorship courses for boys and girls, 10 to 16 years old. These mentoring programs include subject matter that deals with etiquette, life skills, healthy relationships and life blueprint building.

Truthfully, there are a great number of young men and women who are not prepared to walk into a job interview with the right mental or physical fortitude to land a job. Many of our students come to us thinking that it's appropriate to walk into an interview wearing t-shirts and ripped jeans, and then wonder why they can't get a job. We teach them how to look and act professional, even bringing in experts and professionals to speak about career options, financial responsibility, relationship skills and team building.

We also help our kids develop fundamental skills that re-establish the family unit. Back in the day, families would sit down together and have dinner. But more and more, kids are just going to their rooms to eat or sitting at the table staring at their phones, with no communication with their parents or caregivers whatsoever. So, we bring in professional chefs to teach our students how to cook a meal that they can serve to their parents. They serve the food, sit down with their families and eat together.

We teach some simple, common life skills that aren't so common or simple today. Some kids don't have food to cook their parents, or parents to teach them to cook food. We're exposing kids to new things and getting their wheels turning.

Unexpected Speakers We bring in various speakers from the community to talk to our youth. Sometimes we bring in people who may have gone down the wrong path in life, and they talk about what their lives were like when they were in prison or in a gang. We bring these folks in to show the kids that this is not the life they want to pursue. One of our regular speakers was locked up in prison for gangbanging. While he was locked up, his child was killed on the streets. These are the real stories that kids don't get to hear when they're being lured by the streets. We show them the consequences of bad decisions.

These aren't scare tactics, but a way to learn from the experiences of real people. The kids get to see where those paths lead and understand the result of bad choices.

Peer Mentoring

Peer mentoring is basically peer talk, where kids can sit down and talk about their issues with someone around the same age from similar circumstances. It's an interesting concept that has shown amazing results. We partnered with Child & Adolescent Behavioral Health, which provides certified counselors to sit down with the kids. The counselors ask questions like, "What was wrong with your day today? Ok, how do you think we can fix those things?"

It becomes a group discussion, allowing these young men and women to fix their issues by working as a collaborative group.

Tutoring

Nearly every day at the foundation, we offer free tutoring to kids from 3rd to 12th grade in math, language arts, reading and writing. I see kids coming in who are struggling in a subject and they're smiling! They're excited to make progress. We make sure they have snacks, water, juice and whatever they need to feel comfortable while they are learning here. We want to set them up for success in every way possible.

It's Working

The proof is on the faces of these kids and their parents. The proof is in what they're accomplishing. One parent recently approached me with tears in her eyes and gave me the biggest hug. She proceeded to tell me that if it wasn't for our tutoring program, her son would not have passed the 4th grade.

You never really know the level of positive impact you're having on the world until moments like that.

The Be A Better Foundation.

CHAPTER 10

THE NEXT CHAPTER

Irons in the Fire
When I started this foundation, I had no idea I would be where I am today. But now, the only option is to build this thing to greater heights and push this positivity to the next level. This foundation means everything to me. For 20 years, this foundation has been a dream of mine. I know that I'm helping put kids on the right path and saving lives. But I also know that this is just the beginning. In the future, I want to make even more connections, creating more partnerships and allies throughout the community to help us achieve our goals.

For the past few years, this foundation and movement of hope has been building momentum, and I have no intention of slowing down. We are nowhere near the finish line. There are still a lot of kids who need help and guidance. There are still kids turning to the streets instead of turning to academics, positive extra- curriculars and their families.

One kid who still needs help is one too many and I'm preparing to reach them in every way that I possibly can.

Sharpe Vision Publishing
The Indian River Juvenile Correctional Facility recently invited me to talk to their boys. They thought I might be able to change the mentality of some of the boys who are locked up. When I agreed, I had no idea what to expect. These were "bad kids," many who had made some pretty bad decisions.

As I was sitting there talking to these kids, I started to realize that some of them were writers, poets and artists. They had aspirations and things they were passionate about. Suddenly, I began talking about my vision for the future and the publishing company I was creating. They were the first people I told about it. I wasn't there to talk about it, but once I saw the talent in those boys, it made all the sense in the world. I started asking when they got out. Some of them said 2023 and 2024.

"Wow," I said, "Okay, listen, when you get out... and if you can keep your nose clean, and change your lifestyle, and change some of the bad things you're doing... then I will help you create a book, publish it and help you make some money. Maybe this will get you started on doing something you want to do."

One of the kids looked at me in amazement. "That would mean everything to me," he said.

"Okay, that's what's up," I said, "but you have to make the decision to change. If you don't make that decision, I'm not going to let you be a knucklehead and put your name under this thing."

That boy was nearly sharpening his pencil right there. "I'm about to start writing right now. I'll have six books by that time."

"Cool," I said, "I want to see you make it. If that's what will move you forward, let's go. Let's get it."

This year, I launched my book publishing company, Sharpe Vision Publishing. I'm creating a series of books promoting reading, character and positive de- cision-making for young kids. Sharpe Vision will also allow young kids the opportunity to write their very own books to be published.

We have books being published this year.

The Be A Better Me Academy
Many learning environments have grown stale, sticking to outdated methods of instruction. Many years ago, schools started removing the family element from curriculum. Think

about when prisoners go to lunch. They grab a tray, get their food, sit at rectangular tables to eat. That's the same thing they do in schools. We've turned learning into this cookie-cutter institutionalized, static thing.

As far as the foundation goes, one of my next goals is to set up a comprehensive computer lab and transportation for kids whose parents work and can't drive them to and from community programs.

I am also currently working out the details with Canton City Schools to launch the Be a Better Me Academy School in the fall of 2020. Similar to LeBron James' I Promise School, I want to take kids who need a little extra motivation and help them get through school. It's funny that in LeBron and me, you have these two kids from Akron, finding a way to give our youth hope for tomorrow.

Partnering with Akron Public Schools, The LeBron James Family Foundation (LJFF) has designed a new type of school for Akron public school students. LJFF's I PROMISE School is a 1st through 8th grade academic institution that infuses Akron Public School's rigorous curriculum with a STEM, hands-on, problem-based learning focus.

> *I may not have a huge platform like LeBron,*
> *but it's really not the size of your platform.*
> *It's how you use it.*

Like LeBron's school, the Be a Better Me Academy will include group discussions and debates, giving the kids a chance to talk about and reflect on what they've learned each day. We'll also be modernizing some of the tools used and lessons learned throughout the years, tailoring curriculum to the needs of troubled kids today.

The Be A Better Me Academy will be an extension of our foundation. When these kids get out of school, they'll have different extracurricular activities and programs available to them. We'll have washers and dryers for kids to wash their clothes. Seriously, some kids can't wash their clothes. I've seen kids come to school with the same stains on their shirts and shut down out of embarrassment.

The other thing to keep in mind is that every kid learns differently. One of our main goals is to incorporate the things our students want to do in addition to what they need to learn to succeed. There is a school in Atlanta, Georgia called The Ron Clark Academy that has a full production studio, where students can branch out into creative learning. The founders dance as they greet the students each day. This turns into this little soul-train-line-thing, full of smiles and laughter. The kids are happy to be doing what they love. They're excited to learn, have fun and succeed. It's just amazing. The Ron Clark Academy helps kids set and reach goals, which is exactly the type of thing we'll be doing in our academy.

When you're able to find out what the kids want to do and what goals they want to achieve, you'd be surprised to see the difference in them.

My #1 Goal is...
There is still way too much distrust between police officers and the community. On the news, I have seen officers assassinated in their cruiser while they were just eating lunch.

Bad officers are getting involved in unjustified shootings or using excessive force. Good officers are going on calls and getting ambushed. Something needs to be done to mend the relationship between police and communities.

That's one of the main reasons I started the Be A Better Me Foundation. As a police officer, I'm viewed as a person of authority. If I was just a regular Joe Blow around my community, I don't think this would all have the same effect. With an official position of authority, police officers have a big opportunity to reach more people. Some kids are afraid of authority (like I was), but now I know that we can flip those stigmas around and channel that energy in so many other productive ways.

We have a unique opportunity to build hope and trust in our communities. We have a chance to reach so many people and children on a different level.

... Passing the Torch

My vision and goal are to one day open Be A Better Me Foundation centers across the country and have police officers run them. I want to see huge pictures of other officers on buildings throughout the country. I want other officers to be the faces of hope in their neighborhoods and let those communities know that there is a safe place for their children to go and excel.

I'm currently creating a blueprint to give to other officers, so we can expand this movement together. I want to see other officers take my blueprint and build from it, do their thing with it and make it happen. I'd love to see Be A Better Me in cities like Chicago, Cleveland, Detroit, Los Angeles... you name it. I know it's challenging, because there is so much distrust and fury in some of those places. At the same time, Canton's murder rate per capita isn't far from Chicago's, so I know it's possible to expand hope into any community we choose.

We can make it happen.

Just Reach One Kid

All it takes is connecting with just one kid. Then another kid is impacted. And another kid. It creates this domino effect that shows them police officers are human, because they get to see it themselves. They start believing in you and building a bridge of trust.

How do I know? Because it happened to me. We can show kids, and even their parents, that we're here to help make a difference. To serve and protect. To inspire unity and humanity.

There is so much madness in the world, but I truly believe hope will prevail. There's so much more we can do and there's no better time to act than right now. I'm asking for other police officers to join me in supporting a brighter future for us all. We can be the change together.

Together, we can show the world that this is our community and that we are taking it back.

CHAPTER 11

STARTING A NON-PROFIT

All For One
When you're starting a non-profit organization with limited funding, you rely on the support of your community. If you're doing if for the wrong reasons or treating people with disrespect, you are guaranteed to fail and become another one of those foundations sitting by the wayside. I'm so grateful that the people in my community support this foundation. Our supporters know when they donate their money that it's all going to the kids. I pay $25 an hour for our tutors, which gives high school kids an opportunity to make some money. Everything goes to the kids and the community. I don't take a salary and I actually lose money doing this, but I also get the satisfaction of knowing that I'm helping people.

Every venture is different for everyone, but here are a few basic lessons I learned along my journey. Maybe they can help you along yours.

1. *Make the first move.*
   Throughout this journey, I've met some amazing people who want to im- prove their communities and inspire humanity. What I've also learned is that many of these people don't know how to get started building their own cause. All I can say is, go for it and keep pressing on. Starting my foundation was no walk in the park. There have been roadblocks, speed bumps and a lot of barriers of progress. But we put our heads down and carried on. We built this thing because we knew it would inspire change. That's the only way to be successful in anything you do; a relentless pur- suit of excellence.

   Repeat after me, *I will make this happen.*

2. ***Choose your board.***
Creating a powerful board of directors will be your biggest task in de- veloping your foundation. Make sure you pick the right people for your board. Just asking a buddy because he is a cool dude is not necessarily in the best interest of your foundation. Your board should consist of people who share your vision and are willing to invest countless hours to ensure your success. Together you will create your mission statement, bylaws and hold monthly meetings. Your board should be made up of people you trust and believe in. People who trust and believe in you. You will surely need to include someone with a financial background to keep an eye on the budget that's constantly evolving.

3. ***Find your location.***
Maybe you can't get a huge office in the best location at first, so you may need to get creative. As I said before, my foundation was operating out of a church when we first started. Let people in the community know what you're looking to accomplish. There are people out there who may know the perfect place for you to operate out of for cheap, or even free. Check with your local government offices and see if they have available city im- provement grants to fund your new location. You don't necessarily need a building to start an effective non-profit foundation. When you think about it, some of the most successful businesses and causes were started in garages.

4. ***Generate awareness.***
Social media posts, appearances, articles, documentaries, interviews, websites – these are all assets that will help you gain credibility and get the community to stand behind you. The more active you are in your community, the more aware people become of your vision and the more success you will experience. It's so important to network with people who share

your vision. You can often find like-minded people in social media groups, online forums, churches, other foundations and various places within your community.

5. **Start small.**

What you don't want to do is stick your neck on the chopping block by opening an extravagant site where you're struggling to pay the rent each month. For non-profits, running a lean business is critical. Get creative and trade services with others in the community so you get what you need without laying out cash you may not have. Pinch pennies, budget, call in favors. Do everything you have to in order to progress to the next level. If you're struggling with debt and scraping just to stay afloat, you're taking focus away from your cause.

6. **Don't be afraid to ask for help.**

I hate asking people for anything. Back when I was more stubborn, my wife used to get on me and say, "You need to ask somebody!" I would not ask anybody for anything. But what I found out with this foundation is I had to ask for help. I had to humble myself and take a step back. *LaMar, if you want to succeed, you need to ask people for help. You're doing this for the right reasons and people will want to support this cause.* Once I started doing that, everything else started falling into place. You never know who might have the answer you are seeking. You never know who may have the extra capital or charitable donation that they want to put to good use.

7. **Be passionate.**

If you're passionate about a cause, there's a good chance that other peo- ple are too. My organization helps kids and a lot of people relate to that. People are like, "I was that kid! I wish we had this when I was young. Let me help y'all out."

Passion breeds passion. If your supporters, follower, and the people you're helping see that your heart is in it, their hearts will be in it too. Don't start an organization or foundation that you're not ready to get behind 110%. If your cause isn't something that burns inside of you each day, it will fizzle out and be left in ashes.

You're the Main Ingredient

Your character, focus and dedication create the base for your success in everything you do. Starting a non-profit is no exception. If you want to build a non-profit, win a championship, climb Mt. Everest or achieve the highest level of success, you need to be all-in. Surround yourself with the people and things that will help you get there. When you get behind your dream, you will be more than willing to sacrifice time and energy, doing everything it takes to achieve your goal.

And always remember that you are capable of anything. You can do anything.

PART

III

ASSUME THE POSITION

CHAPTER 12

ROLE MODELS

Adulting

I'm not afraid to tell parents when they're messing up. Parents have to be held accountable for their kids and their kids' futures. Kids need parents to push them forward and let them know that they *can* do anything they put their minds to. There are plenty of programs available that teach better parenting strategies. Stark County has the Fatherhood Coalition, which helps fathers become more positive, active participants in their children's lives. They include activities and classes for families, as well. Check in your own community to see what resources could benefit you.

I'm not the perfect father or parent, but I do abide by a few rules that help me connect with my kids and the kids I encounter. Here are a few suggestions based on my experiences as a father, police officer and mentor.

1. ***Stop trying to be your child's best friend.***
   It's not your role and it's not what you're here to do. You're the parent, which makes you responsible for leading by example. I tell parents all the time that if they're out there smoking weed, drinking, partying, having five or six different sexual partners walking in and out of their house – their kids are seeing that behavior as a normal way of life and model the exact behavior. Even if you think it's a good way to live, it's not. I'm not say- ing you must stop all that bad behavior, but if you're going to do it, you have to know when and where to do it. Kids love to model their behavior after their parents. That's why you see generations of families following the same career paths, like attorneys, police officers, doctors, military, etc. It's because children follow the example of their parents. Kids love walking in your foot- steps.

Expose them to healthy and loving habits and watch them follow suit.

It is healthy to have open communication with your kids, but there are par- ents out there who are afraid to be the disciplinarian. There are parents who are afraid to tell their children "No!" Young kids just aren't equipped with the right tools to navigate life on their own terms, by their own rules. They need your guidance and, sometimes, they need a heavy hand.

2. *Get more involved.*
I know of parents who drop their kids off at their grandparents every weekend, so the parents can go party it up. It's irresponsible and imma- ture to put the welfare of your child on hold so that you can go out and kick it. You made the choice to be a parent. You know what you signed up for, so start being a parent and stop acting like a child. It's about them now. Sure, you need to set some time aside to do your own thing, but it shouldn't be every single weekend. Your kids need you.

I know some kids who spend so much time at their grandparents' house that they call their grandparents "mom and dad." What's wrong with that picture? Seriously, it's not okay. When you really think about it, that is crazy.

3. *Learn how to talk to your kids.*
The most valuable lesson I ever had to learn was to listen to my kids, and it took me a long time to get it. It wasn't until I had already raised a few of my kids that I finally realized that I needed to listen to them. When my kids used to tell me things, they'd start off by saying, "Dad, don't be mad."

Before they could even explain, I'd attack them. "What were you think- ing? Are you stupid?"

I was seeing red and approaching everything with anger. That's how I came at my kids and that's how they viewed me. Then I realized that sometimes as a parent, I needed to just shut up and listen to them. Let them finish. Let them tell their story. And then when they tell you the story, you can ask questions without judging them.

Instead of anger, try this: "Were you thinking about what the outcome of your decision would be?"

Try to understand their thought process and then you can correct where they went wrong. That's a much more sustainable way of parenting that opens the lines of communication and connection with your kids for the rest of their lives. There is nothing more rewarding than that type of con- nection, where your kids feel comfortable enough to talk about anything that happens in their lives. One of the greatest opportunities that parents miss out on today is sitting down and eating dinner together as a family.

That means no TV, no phones, no nothing. When you remove those dis- tractions, you'll be surprised how willing children are to open up about their day or the many other situations on their minds.

The relationships I have with some of my older kids are much different than the relationships with my younger kids. My younger kids benefitted from me finally figuring out a better approach to parenting. I still don't have it all figured out, but I can say that I'm getting better at this parent- ing stuff all the time.

4. *Stop and listen.*
Don't judge them, just listen. Can you be cool? I understand that some- times your kids will say something really off the wall that will blow your mind and make you lose your cool and want to jump off a

bridge. I get it. Been there, heard that. I've been there 'woosah-ing' while I'm listening to my kid's ridiculous story. But I've reached a point where I really wanted to understand what my child is thinking. When you start thinking about things that way, it makes it so much easier to build trust in your rela- tionship. If your kids don't trust you, they won't communicate with you. Then you leave them to confide in others on the streets or other people who want to advise them for their own personal gain.

Now, am I still calling them stupid in my head? Absolutely! But I'm not letting them know that. All they see is that we're trying to work this out, as a team.

5. *Show up.*
   I see a lot of kids getting awards or recognition, and their parents are nowhere to be found. You see these kids looking around and searching hopelessly. I understand that parents have to work, but if you can be there, be there. If kids are looking for their parents or loved ones and don't see them, they are distraught and defeated. Your absence is hurting your child. They feel like nobody cares, so why am I doing all this good work. And then we lose a kid who is doing something really, really good, because the people they care about don't care about them.

As parents, we need to make more time for our children.

6. *Monitor media.*
   Social media platforms are powerful tools, but there are good and bad sides to this worldwide phenomenon. Social media platforms have be- come common places for kids to meet up and interact after school. There are dangers of social media, for sure. As a parent, if you're not checking the status of your child online, you're missing the complete picture. For instance, checking to see that your kids arrived safely to the movies or

recreation center. I'm not saying to spy on your children, but you should keep an eye on the things they're spending their time on.

We live in a time where negativity drives many people. Keep an eye on your child's social media accounts and pages to make sure they're not spending their time focusing on and spreading negativity. Many kids show the entire world what they're thinking or feeling on social media but share nothing with their parents. If you're missing that side, it's no- body's fault but your own.

But there's definitely a positive side to using social media. It spreads your message all over the world.

I use social media in hopes to inspire anyone to go out and do something positive within their community. I also use these tools to inspire more officers to get out of their cruisers and become more engaged within the community they work in. People send me messages and ask me to check up on some of the kids I've met, or kids that I know in the community. It's a great tool for what I'm trying to accomplish here.

7. ***Schedule it.***

Schedule time for your kids. I schedule everything and make sure to let my kids know in advance when I have things going on. One of the worst things we do as parents is break promises. We tell our kids that we'll be there and, when life gets in the way, we often sacrifice the things that aren't a priority for us at the time. But a lot of times, those are the things that mean the world to our kids. If you plan and schedule as much as possible, it makes it much easier to be there for them.

I've been in situations where I've called my kids up and asked, "Hey, do y'all want go to Washington for the weekend?" or something like that. Many times, they couldn't make it because they had something going on. I'd make reserva- tions ahead of time and it would end up that a lot of the family couldn't make it.

When you plan, you can say, "How about this? Let's plan [insert event] and everybody clear your schedules for that day." I try my best to schedule time for my kids and grandkids to let them know, "Hey, guys. I'm open this weekend. Maybe we can get something down on our schedules."

Give it a try.

Bad or Misunderstood?
At one of my speaking engagements, I was taking a group of future educators through the following scenario:

"You have little Billy here, who has been cutting up. Now, many of us may label him as a bad kid. But don't assume little Billy is bad. Some of the little Billies I've come across just watched their mom overdose on drugs the night before. Now this kid is at school, trying to be a normal kid. Put yourself in their shoes. You just saw your mom or dad OD on drugs. Are you going to go to work the next day? Are you going to be able to function? Of course not. You're not going to be 100% present based on what you experienced the night before. Before we make a judgement, we need to communicate and find out what's going on with these kids."

I'm regularly called upon to do these types of presentations for parents. On the other end of the spectrum, I also mentor at middle schools, where I work with the kids who spend a lot of their time in in-school suspension. I bring them donuts, breakfast pizzas and stuff like that. Then we sit down and have a chat. I tell them about my life story and explain to them, "You know you don't have to keep getting in trouble all the time. You can make the right choices and be different. You can be anything you want to be."

For some kids, something as easy as this works. And for others, it doesn't.

When I work with these kids, I'm able to connect with them on a peer/mentor level. Everything I try to teach is based on my life experiences. I struggled academically for a while. For whatever reason, I could never understand basic math. I became so frustrated with math that I remember wishing I was dead. I got tired of getting my work back with all these big checkmarks. Wrong. Wrong. Wrong. I was like, "Oh my God. I'm trying my best. Why can't I understand this stuff?"

A part of me wanted to start acting up in class so I didn't have to go to class. If I got in trouble, I wouldn't have to go to sit there and fail at math. Today, I see a lot of kids doing that with all their subjects. Instead of being exposed as someone who can't read, they'd rather skip school. Or they go to school, act up and get kicked out of class. Cutting up is a solution to their problem. That's their solution, just like it was mine.

On Their Level

When I was young, there were many times when I felt like I was just talking to myself, because I had nobody to talk to. I was the oldest of all my siblings, so I didn't really see them as peers who I could talk to about certain things. I didn't talk to most of my friends about my emotions, because I didn't want to appear vulnerable. In bad neighborhoods, you can't show any signs of weakness, because that could get you beat up or killed.

I had to train myself to understand, listen and connect to my own kids. When your kids come home and tell you they accidentally hit a car today, it's a natural response to step in angrily and cut them off before hearing them out. But that only creates a wall between you and them. Now your child is thinking, *I can't even tell my dad, because he's going to flip out.*

You already know you're going to get mad or frustrated at the things your kids do, but you need to be able to control your facial expressions, language and emotions. Calm down, listen and ask questions. Try something like, "What were you thinking when you did this?" or "If you could do it over, what would you do differently?" Sometimes parents don't let their children explain anything. That causes kids to feel like they can't talk to you. So, they go talk to somebody else on the street; someone who's going to give them the wrong knowledge to fit their own agenda.

If your kids don't get the right message at home, they are going to pick up the wrong message on the streets.

Right now, I have eight teenagers in our peer counseling group, because they don't have anybody to talk to about their problems. Every child I come across is going through something. It seems like a hundred people walk right past these kids, but I sense and realize that they may have something going on. I sit there and look at them, watching their body language and other nonverbal cues. The biggest difference between a lot of other adults and I is that I'll approach these kids and say, "What's going on with you?"

That's the thing sometimes. Some kids just want somebody to ask them what's going on. They want to feel like they have somebody to talk to. I ask, "Are you alright? Is everything good? Tell me what's going on." When you do that, the floodgates open, man. If they had more people doing that, maybe it would be easier for them to get on the right track.

It seems like a lot of people just walk by our youth and don't even think to ask them, "How are you? How was your day? What's going on?"

I talk to kids about things that maybe nobody else is telling them.

Little Lady Lessons

One thing I tell young ladies is that they don't have to put themselves out there. Just because a boy asks you for a provocative picture, doesn't mean you need to do that. If they're asking you for that, then that's not the guy for you. If he really respects you, he'll wait. You don't have to put yourself out there. At that age, if you send that kind of picture to a young boy, I'm 120,000% sure he's going to show it to his friends.

These girls look at me with horrified looks on their faces.

"Oh yeah," I tell them, "it's going to happen. If you're not willing to share that with his crew, then don't send it."

A lot of young women haven't thought about those types of things because they just take the word of their peers. The conversations I have with these girls breaks down barriers and helps build trust. But there are many other ways to build that trust.

There's a little 6-year-old girl who I told, "Hey listen, if you can go two weeks without getting a frowny face sticker in class, I'm going to come have lunch with you."

And she did. She held up her side of the bargain, so I met her for lunch at her school and kept my side of the bargain. Her mom was worried that she would act up after our lunch together, so I told the little girl, "If you can go the rest of the year and have two or less frowny faces, then I will make you a character in my children's book."

Her face lit up and she was beyond excited. I really hope she ends up in my book.

My blended family of 11.

CHAPTER 13

FATHER FIGURES

A Twisted Tale of Fatherhood

In our organization, we talk a lot about healthy relationships. Especially relationships with fathers, because that's one of the biggest problems around here. I've been in rooms where kids were asked questions:

"How many of you love your moms? Raise your hands."

All hands raised –

"How many of you love your grandmas?"

All hands raised –

"How many of you love your dads?"

Not even half the hands raised – I picked one kid to dig a bit deeper

Me: "Why don't you love your father?" Kid: "Because my dad doesn't love me."

Me: "Why would you say your dad doesn't love you?"

Kid: "My dad lives two blocks away with another woman and her kids. I don't see him at all."

Kids feel that stuff. Do you want to know why our kids are angry? That's a primary reason right there. A lot of men don't realize the impact they have on their kids, whether they are present or not. But when you ask that question in a room full of children and get those responses, it's eye-opening. It should be common sense to parents that kids want *both* of their parents in their lives.

To you fathers out there, your children need you. Be there. Show up.

Me, my son LaMar Jr., and my dad Lloyd.

Your child sees you as a superhero.
So, act like one.

My Dad, My Superhero

My dad was like my superhero growing up. He played sports. Therefore, I played sports. But when my parents divorced, my dad became consumed with his new situation and placed us on the back burner. I saw him for one weekend every month, but I was mostly with my mom. Sometimes, he would just disappear. He would say he was coming to get me for the weekend, but then he wouldn't show up. I remember standing and looking out the window for hours, waiting there while my mom stood next to me, furious.

I could hear her calling him on the phone in the other room, "You piece of shit. You got your son out here waiting for you."

I'd sit up from the morning until night thinking, *he's going to come get me.* But he didn't. Every time a car passed in front of our house, I would stand up in front of the window with excitement. Those times were heartbreaking. It was like throwing gasoline on the anger that was already bubbling up inside of me. Sometimes when I was playing sports, I'd try to fight other kids. I'd tackle someone and get up, ready to take their head off. Looking back on those times, I now realize that I was letting my resentment take control.

I'd look in the stands and see everybody else's dad, but I'd hardly see mine. My dad rarely showed up until I was in high school. I remember telling my mom I didn't want to go over to him. My anger was based on him not being there, so when I started to see him at my games, I was furious at his inconsistency. I kind of lost hope in him and started feeling like I could care less if he showed up or not.

During my senior year in high school and through my college years, my dad stepped up to the plate and became the father that I needed. When I tore my knee in Kansas, my dad and uncle drove 14 hours to see me through surgery and make sure I was alright. He flew out to Kansas numerous times to hang out and watch me play football. He made the effort to mend our relationship. One day, I sat down and told him how I felt about the past. He listened, which a lot of parents don't do. My dad apologized for his actions and said he was sorry for not being there for us the way he should have when we were kids. After a few tears, hugs and "I love you's," we were good again.

At that point, I got back all those years of affection that I missed as a child. We were able to build the unconditional love that I had lost. We got back to a point where I felt good and finally had my dad the way I needed him. We did everything together – cooking, fishing, family events – you name it. Until, one day, he was gone forever.

Death of Superman

When my dad passed away, it broke my heart. I'll never forget the night I found out my dad was gone. Earlier that day, we were talking on the phone about a menu for our upcoming Family Thanksgiving dinner. I distinctly remember telling my dad that I was going to cook the next day and that he should come and hang out. After talking for a while, he said, "Ok, I love you and I'll see you tomorrow."

I had no idea that this would be the last time I would ever hear him say those words.

When I got the call from my family, I rushed to Akron in total disbelief. I walked into his apartment and there he was lying motionless in his recliner, like he was sleeping peacefully. There were family members, police officers and paramedics in the room. I walked over to him, started rubbing his head and broke down in continuous tears. I vividly remember thinking to myself, *my superhero is gone!*

I was back to loving him the way I did when I was a kid, but I had this gap in my life where I walked around like I didn't need him. It's sad that I lost years of memories with my dad, but I'm grateful that we rekindled that relationship and made it so strong. Even when I felt upset and angry with my dad, he always remained my superhero.

Watching him interact with his grandchildren was priceless. His grandchildren were his world and he was theirs.

An Unwanted Encore

On the night that our family visited the funeral home for my father's final viewing, my mother told me that I needed to go see her mom. My grandma's health had taken a turn for the worse. Later, I headed to my grandmother's residence to spend some time with her. An hour or so into the visit, she passed away before me. Heartbroken can't even describe what I was feeling at that moment. I had lost two incredible people in my life in less than a week.

I know that we are all born to die but losing these two important people at the same time was a cruel blow to my heart.

It's Time to Grow Up

With my dad, I was able to experience both sides of the coin, which has allowed me to relate to kids who have absent fathers or broken families. Nowadays, I have kids coming up to me and saying, "Officer Sharpe, I wish you were my dad."

No kid should have to say that, but that's what they need in their lives. They need structure and stability. They need to know that you're going to be there for them, no matter what. Parents are adults, so it's up to you to make time and put forth the effort to see your kids. Some dads think they are God's gift to all women, fronting like they are super dads, buying material things for their kids and fighting with their child's mom. Some dads are doing everything under the sun except for being a dad, letting their personal agendas overshadow their children, when all they had to do was show up.

You need to get your priorities straight. If you need help, let me drop one little piece of advice that will never let you or your children down:

Your number one default priority is your children.

CHAPTER 14

TO THE YOUTH

Steps For Success

Everything I do is for the kids. I try to teach them lessons to help them grow into the best versions of themselves. People ask me all kinds of questions about parenting and how to communicate with their kids better. I'll be the first one to say that I'm not a perfect parent, but there are some lessons that I try to teach every kid I come across. Maybe you'll have luck teaching your children these lessons. Heck, maybe you'll even have some luck applying them in your own life.

1. *Develop your own positive circle.*

   One of the most important pieces of advice I give to kids is telling them not to put any squares in their circles. Squares are a symbol of negativity and your circle should be nothing but positivity. You don't need that neg- ativity. If someone isn't trying to achieve the same dreams as you, they don't need to be in your circle. You do not need to fit into someone else's group. You don't have to change who you are or sacrifice your morals to fit in. A lot of kids say, "But that's my friend." I totally understand that, but if your friend is doing something that is going to cost you or affect you negatively, then they aren't being a good friend to you. Heartache, drama, legal problems – you just don't need that negativity in your life.

   Don't let other people pull you down because you want to be accepted.

   That's not the type of acceptance that you need in your life to be a good person. If they're really your friend and know that you're trying to be better and do something positive for yourself, they won't bring that neg- ativity into your life. If you refuse to commit crimes, do drugs or drink alcohol, and someone dogs you or talks bad about you for that, then they are not your friend. True friends will respect your decisions. Real friends want you to be better. Even if they're going to go do that kind of stuff, they shouldn't try to force you into doing something you don't want to do. I understand that a lot of kids feel peer pressure. We live in a time where everybody sees this lifestyle on social media and want to live it. But that thuggish ruggish lifestyle that's portrayed on social media isn't as glamorous as it appears to be.

The coolest people, celebrities and icons out there are the ones who are lifting up the energy of others.

2. ***Focus on the things you like to do.***
A lot of kids don't know what they want to do and aren't aware that they can make a life doing what they love. What do you like to do? Do you like to use your hands? Do you like to be creative? Do you like numbers? Once we find out what the kids like to do, it makes it really simple to help them build a solid life blueprint. I tell them, "Here. These are some things that might make sense for you to do. You can do more, but here are some things that come to mind. Do you like anything here? You don't? Okay, well let's look over here because these things fall into the same category. All these things that you like to do, pick your top five. Okay, now here are some things that you need to focus on to make your dream a reality."

Once we establish a baseline and destination, we can start to develop the life blueprint.

3. ***Develop a life blueprint.***
I spend a great deal of time helping these kids develop their character. I ask them who they are as a person and what do they want to be. Once we know who we are and

who we want to be, we can design the blueprint for their lives that will bridge that gap.

At some point in time, I had to develop a life blueprint for myself, but a lot of these kids don't do that. They are just living in the moment. They're not thinking about what they're going to do when they turn eighteen and have to go live in the real world. They aren't thinking about what they're going to do with themselves. They're just living for the here and now, and that's one of the things that I try to work on.

I say things like, "You have to develop a blueprint. What is it that you like to do? You like to use your hands. Okay. Let me show you some things where you can use your hands. You like computers? You like video games?"

Whatever it is that they like. I help them see that they can create and make their own path, career and life, doing things they love. I don't think a lot of kids understand that they have options to do what they love. They don't think outside the box or have someone to guide them to opportu- nities and goals. When I realized that's what they needed, I realized that my gift is the ability to think like a kid. Thinking back to how I was and seeing these kids today, I can relate to them. And that makes it really easy for me to go in and talk to them.

Create your life blueprint by asking yourself, "What do I need to do?"

You're on a personal journey to a specific destination. What are the right things you need to do each day to reach that destination? Where are you trying to go and what do you need to take with you? Sometimes on your journey, you need to travel light. You don't need to take all the bad lug- gage with you. Maybe you had a bad upbringing and that's okay, but that happened in the past and you can't let it affect your present and future. Kids (and adults) need to understand that they can leave that baggage behind. You don't need it. It will only weigh you down. It will only bring you down. So why take it with you?

I tell people, "Hey, listen, my circumstances were A, B & C. Instead of do- ing A, B & C as a quick cash solution, I decided to make a plan for myself. I developed an X, Y & Z plan, so now I don't have to worry about all the other stuff in-between."

And that's when they start to get it.

"That's why I'm here today.
I could have easily made the choice to work the streets
for the quick dollar. I could have made the choice to be
a criminal and been that guy locked up or dead, right?
Absolutely. I could be that guy.

When I tell kids that, they start looking at themselves and going, "I need to get my life together."

When you see kids who have a life blueprint, you start to see more focus. You see the bad behaviors that they had in the past slowly start to dimin- ish. You can truly see it.

We help young men and women develop a blueprint for life. When I say blueprint, I mean we tell them that it's just like building a house. You wouldn't build the roof first, so our blueprint starts with the foundation. That's what we try to do with our youth, have them start a life blueprint at the foundation.

How do I explain it to these kids?

How would you go about building a house? Just throw the windows up? It doesn't work that way. You've got to start with a foundation and work your way up.

I ask the kids what they like to do and where they want to be. I say, "Great. Okay, let's get it and build it from the foundation. Then, we're going to put all the accessories on and make it nice and good."

4. **Work on your family relationships.**
Plain and simple, you need to develop and maintain a strong relation- ship with your family. Some kids treat their friends better than they treat their parents and family. Friends may come and go, but your family is forever. As you go out into the world on your personal journey, you will sometimes stumble. And sometimes, you might need somebody to lean on. Guess what? Some of your so-called friends aren't going to be there. It's going to be your parents and your family who are going to be there. So, keep those relationships strong and tight. When you fall back and they're there to catch you, they're going to push you forward so you can keep going. Some of your "friends" will let you fall. Some may even laugh at you and enjoy seeing you fall. Your family is going to support you and get you back on the right track.

5. **Be kind and help others.**
I tell kids we need more kindness in this world. Every time you turn around, you see something negative. It's okay to help other people. So many of these kids think they have to be mean or carry a scowl on their face to protect their image. But the toughest of us are the ones who will help somebody else.

6. **Always push forward.**
Never stop becoming the best version of yourself. Nobody is perfect, but if you're getting better all the time, you will find success, happiness and fulfillment. Always remember that your current circumstance is not your identity.

HARD EVIDENCE

There have been many, many times where I asked myself, *what am I really doing here? Is this thing even working?* But every time I doubted myself, I could look around and see another kid who was becoming a better person from the things I was trying to do. This kid was getting better grades. That kid stopped causing trouble. That kid started going to school for a change.

I know I say it a lot, but each one of us has the potential and responsibility to be the change we want to see in the world. Just think if everybody did that. Just think if ten people you know did that together. Think of all the positive companies, causes and impacts that have come from groups with less than ten people. Just by being the change and being proactive, you could be the spark needed to start a long-lasting fire of positive change in your community and the world.

It really troubles me that a lot of people feel immobilized, like they can't help or change anything. It's very frustrating to me, because it's so far from the truth. You need to take a step forward and act. Be proactive. Go to any non-profit that you believe in and get involved. Ask them what they need. You can't sit back and expect everything to just work itself out. The key is to get started. If you don't make the effort, you'll never get the results you want to see in any aspect of your life. If I never would have started passing out candy to kids, I wouldn't be here today. Just move, no matter what comes along.

Yeah, I doubted myself and my purpose. But the evidence and the community kept growing all around me. Here are a few success stories that I'm grateful to have been a part of.

SUSPECT #9: J'Mon Wells

One of "my kids," J'Mon, grew up in a bad neighborhood here in Canton, Ohio. It was a bad situation. This kid reminded me of myself. He was a great athlete who I coached in football. I took a special interest in him and tried to keep an eye on him, because I knew he was about to make some bad decisions and mistakes. I used to sit outside of his residence while I was working on my police shift. I remember at first, he avoided making eye contact with me. Even though he knew me, in those neighborhoods, it's not cool to be talking to the police. I sat there and I'd wave to him and he'd come over and talk to me.

"Why are you sitting outside my house?" He'd say.

"Because I want to make sure that you're safe. I want to make sure nothing happens over here. Plus, if I'm sitting here and you thought about doing something stupid, you ain't going to do it," I'd tell him.

J'Mon straightened up and built a life blueprint. And guess what? He's now a deputy sheriff. He won Massillon's scholarship for peace officer training. He's got a daughter and it's all just amazing. I'm so proud of this dude and now I'm watching him do the same thing I'm doing with kids in his area. I am beyond proud of him.

That's when you know this thing is working, when you hear success stories like that.

J'mon Wells

SUSPECT #32: Eric Puckett

I remember a lot of kids who passed in and out of the doors of the detention center during my tenure there. Among those incarcerated kids was Eric. This young man came in with a huge chip on his shoulder. Eric was a very troubled teen in need of hope and guidance. He was bouncing around from different group homes at that time, running away until the police would catch up to him. He was a tough kid and the things he was going through were making him even tougher. Like many kids in a detention center, Eric thought that he could scare me and possibly get special privileges while he was incarcerated. This tactic may have worked for him before, but it wasn't going to work with me.

After Eric broke a facility rule, I had to take his belongings away from him. Eric got angry and challenged me. When I took his personal belongings, Eric came after me to fight. I physically restrained him and took him to the ground until he calmed down. You're probably thinking, why would a child try to attack a 6'6", 275 pound former collegiate linebacker? When youth are troubled, they often become accustomed to making poor choices. He made a poor choice that day. However, I did not hold a grudge against Eric. Instead, I took the opportunity to explain to him that he was a good kid who was making poor decisions. I saw myself in Eric. We developed a close relationship and I always made sure to give him some positive words whenever our paths crossed.

Years after our run-in at the detention center, I was out with some kids doing my community policing thing and guess who I run into? Eric!

Eric didn't just turn into a good man, he turned into a great father, as well. He is now a very proactive, present father in his children's lives. I'm so proud of him. Each and every morning, I see him walking his kids to the bus stop or all the way to school. He has a good head on his shoulders, he's never been to prison and, more importantly, he is alive to experience life.

Eric Puckett

A CALL TO ARMS

"Whatever affects one directly, affects all indirectly."

- Dr. Martin Luther King Jr.

Officer Sharpe Mania!"

Be A Better You

I know I've said it a lot in these pages, but you have to be the change you want to see in the world. We must get involved and start worrying about more than our own families. We worry about our own so much. *"I'm only worried about my family and what's mine."* Okay, I understand that because I worry about my family, too. But I also worry about this community and your family. And his family. And her family. And these kids.

Sometimes, I'm actually afraid for the future. In today's world, it's all about "Me." Everybody worries about themselves. People get so self-involved with the grind that they stop worrying about other people. They worry about themselves so much that it's toxic. They don't worry about the future, outcomes of their decisions or how they could impact the bigger plan.

Right now, it feels like we're going backwards.

If I was just worrying about myself, I'd be working off-duty as a security guard at a bar or Walmart on my off time. That's how policemen make their money, but I don't have that luxury of extra time anymore. I'd love to make that kind of money to afford things that I want, but I'm living paycheck to paycheck and giving my time. If you're not helping others, or making yourself better so you can help others, you need to wake up. It's up to us to lift one another. When you're only worried about yourself, bad energy comes landing right on your front door

– stuff that you figured would never affect you.

You get what you put out into this world. Your aim should be to spread kindness, hope and love. I don't see how anyone could argue that point, but there are plenty of parents out there who aren't putting out the right energy or teaching their children this simple lesson.

We all have to be proactive and take responsibility for this world.

We are all on a personal journey to become the person who we want to be. Travel light. Don't carry useless, negative baggage with you.

Be The Change

My goal is to make myself better first. Then I can start to make everybody around me better. I honestly think that should be the goal of us all. If you want to help people, you need to help yourself first. I know that when I make myself better, I can make everyone around me better. When everyone around me is better, they're going to turn around and make everyone around them better. It's a continuous cycle of positivity.

If we all did that, we wouldn't have all this negativity and bad energy going around. Leadership by example is a proven concept and it starts inside of us. When we are not good ourselves, we can't make others better. If we're out here doing all these bad things, how are we going to help other people be better? Within ourselves, we need to make the decision to make this place better and take the first step. I challenge you to become a better you, the best version of you.

A better you makes the world a better place.

Become the change you want to see in the world at
www.lamarsharpe.com
www.beabetterme.org

Get a free download of LaMar's hit documentary,
"When A Community Chooses To Come Together"
directed by Rashaud Polk at www.lamarsharpe.com.

ISBN: 978-1-7340740-1-7 (Paperback)

Library of Congress Control Number: 00000000000

Written by LaMar Sharpe & Aaron McMahon
Front cover images by Joe Albert.
Book and creative design by Corey Oesch.

Printed by Sharpe Vision Publishing in
the United States of America.

First edition 2019.

Sharpe Vision Publishing
525 Market Ave N
Canton, Ohio 44702

www.lamarsharpe.com

Made in the
USA
Lexington, KY